Be Bold in the Broken

"Mary Lenaburg has a rare gift of holy hospitality, and I couldn't put this book down. With each turn of the page, I found myself feeling at home in her vast heart and boldly embracing new facets of my own brokenness and beauty. What a gift this book will be to so many!"

Carrie Schuchts Daunt
John Paul II Healing Center presenter
Author of *Undone*

"Mary Lenaburg's life has been filled with many shake-you-to-your-core moments, yet she kept pushing forward. How? The quiet voice of God was always with her, even when she wasn't ready to listen. A faith and life chock-full of courageous moments strung together with all the joy, sorrow, and hope this world has to give—that's what you'll experience in the pages of *Be Bold in the Broken*."

Allison Gingras
Founder of *Reconciled to You*
Host of *A Seeking Heart* podcast

"The first time I saw Mary Lenaburg she was on stage telling stories. I never imagined that in *Be Bold in the Broken* she would take her storytelling to a whole new level! Every chapter made me feel like Lenaburg was sitting next to me with a cup of coffee, and her bathing-suit shopping story had me yelling, '*Preach it, sister!*' She has a gift of transforming the everyday into great stories that draw her readers closer to God."

Liv Harrison
Creator of the Genius Catholic Women's Conference

"Doesn't every woman ask herself if she's enough, if she can do more to fit in, and how much she has to sacrifice to do it? If you've ever asked yourself those questions, I promise you will find yourself nodding in agreement with Mary Lenaburg. *Be Bold in the Broken* made me feel seen, laugh out loud, and tear up in solidarity. Lenaburg doesn't shy away from the hard things, the hard moments, or the hard realizations. Through her words, I felt a loving embrace from Jesus reassuring me that I am worthy and needed no matter the battles I've fought, and I know you will too."

Kathryn Whitaker
Author of *Live Big, Love Bigger*

"Through equal doses of humility and truth, Lenaburg shares from the heart what it means to discover who you truly are and how walking in this truth really can change your life. I cried, nodded in agreement, and laughed out loud. This book makes me feel seen and understood, and it encouraged me to seek treasure where it can be found."

Rachel Balducci
Catholic author, speaker, and cohost of *The Gist* on CatholicTV

"In her characteristic style and distinctive voice, Lenaburg invites us all to own our own stories, to embrace who we are, and to let God use us for his divine purpose. This book will encourage you and challenge you to find the courage to love yourself as exactly who you are and come to know how deeply God loves you too. A great read filled with humor and insight, this is a book we all need to remind us of how deep his love for us really is."

Colleen C. Mitchell
Author of *Who Does He Say You Are?*

How I Found My Courage and Purpose
in God's Unconditional Love

Be Bold in the Broken

Mary E. Lenaburg

Ave Maria Press AVE Notre Dame, Indiana

_____

Founded in 1865, Ave Maria Press is a ministry of the United States Province of Holy Cross.

www.avemariapress.com

Paperback: ISBN-13 978-1-64680-039-1

E-book: ISBN-13 978-1-64680-040-7

Cover image © gettyimages.com.

Cover and text design by Katherine Robinson.

Printed and bound in the United States of America.

Library of Congress Cataloging-in-Publication Data
Names: Lenaburg, Mary (Mary E.), author.
Title: Be bold in the broken : how I found my courage and purpose in God's unconditional love / Mary E. Lenaburg.
Description: Notre Dame, Indiana : Ave Maria Press, 2021. | Summary: "In this book, Mary E. Lenaburg finds the courage to boldly accept God's unconditional love and become the woman God called her to be while exploring the lessons she learned from her own brokenness along the way to discovering her true identity and mission in the unfailing love of God"-- Provided by publisher.
Identifiers: LCCN 2020045235 | ISBN 9781646800391 (paperback) | ISBN 9781646800407 (ebook)
Subjects: LCSH: God (Christianity)--Love. | Identity (Psychology)--Religious aspects--Christianity. | Courage--Religious aspects--Christianity. | Christian women--Religious life.
Classification: LCC BT140 .L46 2021 | DDC 231/.6--dc23
LC record available at https://lccn.loc.gov/2020045235

For my dad, William Joseph Green. Thank you for teaching me to embrace my boldness, to never quit on life, and to love God above all else. You were the first man I ever loved and who loved me back. Save a dance in heaven for me.

For my Jerry. Thank you for loving me just as I am and for making me laugh every single day. I would not be who I am without you by my side. I love you with my life.

For you, dear reader. Know you are enough, right now in this moment, because God makes it so. You are seen and loved by the Father, who is delighted with you. Let him love you, friend. It makes all the difference.

Contents

Foreword

LEAH DARROW

Where are you?
—Genesis 3:9
What are you looking for?
—John 1:38

Questions from God require a long pause. And a response.

I wonder what your answers are to these questions. Where is *your* heart? Is it far from God, or closer than it's ever been? What are you looking for? Healing? Courage? Purpose?

You've picked up this book for some reason, even if that is not completely clear to you now. You may have experienced your fair share—or not-so-fair share—of brokenness. Perhaps you are hoping for inspiration to become a more fully integrated person. Or maybe you're looking for a friend, a companion who can show you how to become the woman God made you, even if that means being *bold*.

I've never met anyone who feels bold when they're broken. Yet here we are, with Mary Lenaburg's mandate to *be bold* and stories of how she discovered what God's unconditional love could mean not only for her but also for us. Because let's face it: the intricate relationship of brokenness and boldness is one only God can forge. God desires and seeks out the brokenhearted. Each of us has her own story of brokenness.

To me, the word "brokenness" is a trigger train that runs back to my past. It usually drops me off at one stop: New York City, April 2, 2005. Then, I lay under my covers, sobbing in despair at the next few steps I thought I had to take to end my pain and the pain I was causing others . . . my very life. To say that I was broken would have been an understatement. I was truly in pieces.

Just moments prior, I had walked out of a photoshoot, and ended my modeling career. I did that because I realized that my life *must* have more meaning than what other people or our culture said or dictated. I was bold in that moment, and it felt good. But shortly after I got home, I began to doubt God's love and mercy. I began to doubt God. The enemy knew me; he knew my ache and my need and sought to fill it with lies and destruction.

Still, our God saves, my friends. He redeems all that is broken; "he heals the brokenhearted and binds up their wounds" (Ps 147:3, NRSV). Nothing short of a miracle happened next. God used a journalist with breaking news across my TV to jolt me out of my stupor with the words, "It is official, we've just received word, Pope John Paul II has died." My mind and heart immediately heard the Holy Father's famous and familiar words, "Be not afraid!"

I climbed out of my bed, ignored the booming inner voice of shame and despair, and called my dad. "If you don't come and get me, Dad, I'm going to lose my soul." A long pause made me nervous, but when my father spoke he said, "OK, baby, I'm coming to get you." God's grace was at work to bring me back home to him. My first stop was reconciliation. It didn't feel bold, but it was. God gave me the grace of boldness to ask for forgiveness, accept it, and believe it. For me, being bold in the broken looked like a person on their knees asking God for mercy.

"The LORD is near to the brokenhearted, and saves the crushed in spirit" (Ps 34:18, NRSV). The Lord saves the crushed in spirit! Crushed, smashed, broken—whatever you may be or have been, the Lord saves.

It's hard to witness or listen to the brokenness of others. It's harder still to see and accept brokenness in ourselves. God doesn't see things the way we do. But we can learn to see ourselves the way God sees us. That is what this book will help you to do. The Lord reveals the beauty of broken things and people. As Ven. Fulton Sheen said, "Broken things are precious. We eat broken bread because we share in the depth of our Lord and His broken life. Broken flowers give perfume. Broken incense is used in adoration. A broken ship saved Paul and many other passengers on their way to Rome. Sometimes the only way the good Lord can get into some hearts is to break them."

All of those moments in life that just didn't turn out the way we thought they would or should are opportunities for God to break in and redeem. With his healing grace, God leaves his mark of boldness: the ability to see who we are, broken, but beloved—belonging to him.

While our brokenness reveals our need for God, our boldness reveals our surrender to his mercy. The beauty of boldness is that it comes from the One who is bold but never broken. And the grace of being bold in the broken is a reminder of the One whose unconditional love saves us and makes all things new.

This book will be the balm many souls need right now. May your path through brokenness always be bold.

longing for love

Every human heart (including mine) longs for love and meaning. We want to be recognized as special and to be valued exactly as we are. And there's nothing wrong with that, because God gives each one of us his love and a unique and holy purpose. But there's a catch. We can't just *believe* that God loves us. We have to *accept* God's love—and that takes courage, especially when you know how broken you are.

I'm writing this introduction over New Year's, and I have spent days reevaluating my life, with all of my mistakes appearing in Technicolor. (I could be watching football and eating nachos, but that would be too easy.) The problem with this kind of internal analysis (not fueled by holiday junk food) is that the deeper I sink into my head, the more sure I become that no one could ever love me.

Especially God.

Maybe you're nodding along because you've been there—or are there—yourself. Or maybe you're a bit confused because you thought I'd be able to convince or at least reassure you that God loves everyone unconditionally, including you. He does, by the way, love you unconditionally. But hearing that isn't enough, is it?

For a very long time, I was afraid to accept the free gift of God's unconditional love because I was sure I didn't deserve it. Doubt and fear threw me into a no-win cycle

Be Bold in the Broken

of self-destruction. So even though I wanted to be seen, I hid my brokenness. Even though I desired to be known, I kept trying to be someone I wasn't. And even though I longed to be loved, I kept everyone—including God—at a distance. I hid behind masks and facades so that people would love me. But guess what? All of that just made it harder for me to actually receive love or truly embrace my God-given purpose.

Who knew?

I'm pretty sure you know who did, but it took me years to find out.

The Dressing Room

Trying to figure out who I am in God's eyes has been similar to my worst dressing-room experience ever. You know the drill. There's an important social event, and I have "nothing to wear." I go shopping and walk among the racks of brightly colored apparel, choose multiple pieces from the abundant selection, and head in. Immediately I am hit with those nasty fluorescent lights that make me look like I am battling typhoid fever. They remind me of all the people who judge how I dress, what makeup I wear, what charity I support, and what political party I vote for.

The humming of those fluorescents, however, hides something more insidious: Satan's whisper that I'm better off being invisible. Then the real test begins. While I'm drawn to the bold dresses in bright colors or vivid patterns, I know I'll be the only woman in the room not wearing a little black dress. And one thing I desperately need is to fit in with this group of women. I pass by the red dresses—a sequined gown in particular—and pick out one I know will fit. It's a black dress that would've been killer on Audrey Hepburn. And . . . it fits. Well, sort of. It's a safe choice that I know I can wear again—not too short, not too long, not too tight. In this dress, I'll fit in. I'll be accepted and acknowledged as one of the group. I'll be seen as the ideal wife, a perfect complement to my dapper spouse.

I wear it for the event and feel like an imposter the entire evening. Despite getting some compliments, I am lost in a sea of black. My inner diva is screaming because I look like everyone else. And while I fit in—which is exactly why I chose this dress—I'm mad and sad because I know I do not truly belong.

Then the room goes quiet, and I look toward the front of the ballroom. A woman is standing there, her hand on her husband's arm. She's in a red gown—the same sequined gown I passed by in the store. Heads turn, women whisper, and the music pauses.

And I'm wracked with jealousy.

The music starts again, but all I can hear are those darn fluorescents humming in my mind.

I ask myself why I am so upset. I *chose* a dress that helped me fit in, a dress that guaranteed I would be accepted. Yet, in the process, I gave up part of myself and hid who I really am. In trying to be approved by those whose opinions mattered to me, I became someone else. I gave away the red sequined dress for the safe LBD.

The same mental process happens when we seek our identity anywhere other than in the Lord. We pick up dress after dress, trying to be accepted and acknowledged. We choose the dress that worked for Janet and Susie and then resent it when it doesn't work for us.

For years I kept trying on dresses that fit people I wanted to emulate but ignored the ones that were perfect for me. Those seemed too bright, too bold, too much. They were the kinds of dresses that would separate me from the group. I listened to the voice that kept repeating the lie that I would never be enough as I was. I just wanted to fit in, but even then, God was calling me to stand out and be the bold and dynamic woman he created me to be.

In the red sequined gown.

And he calls you to do the same.

Red sequins may not be your thing, and that's fine. But do you know what color *your* dress is? Are you still trying on all the wrong things and walking out into life with something that doesn't fit or express who you really are? This book is an invitation to come into the dressing room with me because a friend is so much better than those three-way mirrors.

What God Wants

In my travels, I am often asked, "What does God want of me?"

It's a simple answer really: holiness. That's it. And now you can put this book down and move on with your life, or you can choose to read on and witness my journey to understanding what holiness is. It's quite the adventure. A tale filled with gossip and drama, loneliness and rejection, failure and false humility. Sounds exciting, right? I wish I could say it was, but mostly it has been an internal struggle to allow God to transform my heart into something more like his. Remember, God not only wants holiness of you; he also wants holiness *for* you.

Allowing God to do his work in me is not an easy task for a stubborn, willful woman whose life motto has always been, "I just want everyone to love me and do things my way." Humility is my middle name.

For the majority of my life I have acted out of the wounds of my childhood. It wasn't until I realized that I was inflicting that woundedness onto the ones I held closest to my heart that I even considered living my life differently. Sometimes sharing isn't caring.

Change was coming, but first I had to realize that God's love isn't something we can earn; it's a gift that must be received. And I couldn't do that until I recognized two basic truths. The first is that we belong to God alone. The second is that we must seek to understand who we are in God's eyes, not anyone else's, in order to discover who God made us to be.

So, who are you in God's eyes? You'll never know until you can accept God's absolutely unconditional love, allowing it to mold you into the person he made you to be. You'd think something so simple would be easy—it isn't. It takes courage to receive God's love. I'm hoping that sharing the crazy stories of my life will help you find yours. In this book we'll explore my failures as I came to know who I am, whose I am, and my God-given calling. And trust me—my failures *were* epic (like the stuff that internet memes are made of). So, let the ~~bloodletting~~ storytelling begin.

CHAPTER 1

Measuring Up and Fitting In

‿◡

I never had a girl tribe. You know the kind of friends that strut down the center of the hallway at school and just own who they are. Like in *Mean Girls*, but not so mean. I always wanted to be part of a group like that but really struggled to make friends. Always too loud or too excited, I was impatient and made brash decisions like cutting my hair in the fourth grade so I didn't have to deal with a ponytail during basketball practice. Unfortunately, my mother took me to the same Greek barber as my six brothers, and I ended up looking like Brad Pitt in *A River Runs through It*. What worked for Brad did not work for me.

I stumbled though junior high and high school joining this club and that, always searching for a safe place to land. Then I met and married my husband, and we began the great adventure of being a Navy family. I thought I had finally found my tribe. These women came from all walks of life, with so many different backgrounds and experiences, but were now sharing a common focus of keeping the home fires burning while our husbands served our country.

As I settled into base housing in New England, I made friends with two of my neighbors, Becky and Miss J. They were smart, capable women, new moms like me, and we were all in this life together. We spent playdates together, took walks, shopped, and babysat each other's children for date nights and quick commissary trips. Becky was low-key and always so kind and accepting of everyone. Her door was always open, and you knew you were welcome in her home, laundry on the couch or not. Miss J was a bit more driven and single-minded.

Getting Ahead

In those days women sometimes wore their husband's rank to establish their place in the very large pool of humanity. Both Miss J and I fell into that trap, but I was the low woman on the totem pole. She and Becky were both well-educated professional women before choosing to stay home with their young children. I was not. They were both confident and comfortable with who they were. I was not. Their homes were neatly organized with newish furniture and beautifully appointed knickknacks. Mine was a Goodwill/Salvation Army mash-up with a splash of college dorm life for color. I wanted to be like them, self-possessed and keen. Instead I felt small and unseen. So I decided to do something to change that.

I have never been known for my patience or discernment skills. I rarely took the time to sit with God and ask him to weigh in or guide me. I'm a bit of a steamroller, known for leaping without being too concerned about where I will land, and I also don't do anything in half measure. So when I decided to make some changes, I went all in. It was *Extreme Makeover: Home Edition*, Mary style.

I successfully ran for the position of Squadron Wives Club president, started volunteering at the little Catholic church in town, and finally joined the local YMCA to begin transforming my mom bod. More than anything, I wanted to be able to stand confidently beside these fabulous women at any given social event and not feel "less than."

Because I couldn't get past the comparisons I was sure everyone else was making, I began chasing the image of someone I wished I was without asking for directions or input from the One who made me who I am. In that moment, I was telling God that he had made a few mistakes with the circumstances of my life and that I was more than happy to fix it for him.

So helpful, don't you think? Mary telling the God of the Universe that she could make life better than he could? My lack of humility still stuns me.

Now I can feel y'all shaking your heads in a collective *Desperate much, Mary?* Yes. Very much so. I had spent my whole life being "Joe Green's daughter" or the sister of <insert-random-sibling's-name-here>, or my favorite: "She's a Green." Never Mary, Mary Beth; I was just an add-on, attached to seven other siblings and two parents who were known by everyone and their brother. The only time I was seen for just being me was when I was given detention for something I had done in order to, you guessed it, be seen.

So like Eve in the garden of Eden who decided she knew better than God, I grasped for any apple I saw hanging from the tree of social acceptance. I strived for the image of perfection that would lead to recognition by others on base. When someone complimented me in some way, I simply blazed the trail to future downfall with false humility and pride and said, "Oh, it's nothing."

Determined to do whatever it took to be accepted, I learned how to make jam to compete in a local farmers market contest with a cash prize so I could purchase new fabric to make a dress for an upcoming Dining In event. I didn't win, but I did end up selling my jam to my fellow wives and neighbors, which did earn the money I needed for that new dress. I upped my primitive baking game and bartered my famous apple crumble pie for instruction in how to quilt and make decorative sofa pillows, since I couldn't afford the Pottery Barn ones I lusted after. I believed that if I could present everything just so, there would be no room for rejection.

Gossip Girl

Over time, what started out as a lovely friendship with Miss J became a major competition. I'm not sure when the tide turned. Maybe it was when my son bit her son on the playground in a toddler tussle over a toy fire truck. Maybe it was when I announced a squadron fundraising idea, and then two weeks later she and her squadron wives decided to do the same thing. Instead of taking that as a compliment, I was offended that she had stolen my awesome idea. (Forget that I got the idea from another squadron who had done it the year before.) Maybe it was when she and several of our neighbors went to the zoo one day and decided not to invite me or Jonathan. It was a double rejection of both me and my toddler son. That sucked me into a swirling vortex of fear and self-loathing.

One Thursday afternoon, Miss J and I were going to watch a pay-per-view concert of the Judd's together. We were both huge country-music fans, and the Judd's were giving their farewell concert. She had cable; I did not. Our husbands were out on training missions, so we had planned to put the kids to bed and watch the concert together.

Before I went to Miss J's house for the concert, however, I took a call from a mutual friend. As we talked about who was doing what, I discovered that Miss J had been recognized for a charity project, and I had not. In the span of a breath, I was consumed by jealousy and anger. Mary's *ugly* showed up, and I spoke against Miss J and her character.

My envy of Miss J erupted, and the words of gossip and jealousy that flowed out of my mouth in that moment still make me want to vomit. When Mary goes dark, it's straight to the pits of hell, friend.

When I hung up I felt vindicated for all of the thirty seconds it took before the realization of what I had actually said landed on me. I had given into my own pride and neediness. This wasn't who God called me to be, not by a long shot.

Remember how Adam and Eve hid after they ate the apple and saw that they were naked? I tried to hide as well. Unfortunately for me, this mutual friend cherished her friendship with Miss J and called to tell her every horrible word I had said. Later, when I showed up at Miss J's house to watch the concert, not knowing that she'd already spoken to our other friend, I was greeted with righteous anger and tears of betrayal—the kind portrayed brilliantly on *The Real Housewives of Orange County* or by the Kardashians. I stood there trying desperately to dig out of the hellish hole I had dug for myself, failing miserably. Respect was lost, trust was broken, and a friendship was destroyed. She even slammed the door in my face.

All because I couldn't stop comparing myself to other people. Not even friends.

Instead of just doing my best to be a good friend, I listened to the lie that Satan had been whispering into my heart for months: in order to be seen, I had to be better than everyone else. I had given into my own lack of appreciation for the gifts and talents God had given me and had tried to outdo the gifts God had given to others.

I immediately went to Becky's and poured out every horrible vile lie I had spoken and asked her what to do. She allowed me to cry on her sofa and bemoan my idiocy without ever judging me herself, and she simply said, "You have to make it right, Mary. You'll figure it out." Wiser words were never spoken. I went back home and cried myself to sleep.

The next morning, I woke up with a crying hangover, still unsure of how I was going to make things right with Miss J. I started to fold the laundry, and as I picked up a pair of Jerry's sweat socks, I was transported in time to another tragic tale of Mary grasping for acceptance and recognition.

Yes, I'd been in this horrible, humiliating spot before.

Tumbling Sweat Socks

Middle school is hard. That's just a fact of life. The hormones, the growth spurts, and the increase in pressure to perform academically are a lot to handle. I know it may come as a shock to you, but I did not handle it well. Not well at all. I was five feet eight in the sixth grade and taller than all but three people in my class. I was a giraffe named *Awkward*. But that didn't make me any less desperate for attention.

The Catholic school I attended had a football team with no cheerleaders. When I was in sixth grade, that all changed. The upcoming cheerleading tryouts were *the* topic of conversation, and all I remember thinking about was how unathletic I actually was. I could run, maybe even jump decently. But splits, backflips, or toe touches? Nope. Still, I was determined. I wanted a tribe, and I just knew that this was my way in. I went to the library, got a book on cheerleading, and practiced in my backyard every day after school.

It was not pretty, and my brothers thought it was hysterical. They kept telling me I looked like a circus clown. They weren't wrong. I fell more times than I could count and barely made it six inches off the ground. But I kept trying. I watched every college football game for weeks just to see what the cheerleaders were doing. One thing about me, good or bad, is that when I commit to something, I am all in.

Tryout day arrived, and I couldn't eat my lunch at school because I was so nervous. I wanted to make that team more than anything. I knew that once that happened,

I was going to be somebody. They would know my name. Not my brothers' or my father's. *Mine.*

As the girls lined up to do the practice cheer and tumbling run, I noticed two things. First, everyone wore graphic cap-sleeved T-shirts and Adidas shorts circa 1978. I wore one of my brother's hand-me-down solid-white T-shirts and Kmart shorts. That second thing? Every girl there had a chest. Every. Single. One. I was as flat as a cardboard box. Somehow my mind twisted that realization into the thought that in order to be a cheerleader, I needed a chest. I had to conform to everyone else around me. Like immediately—steamroller Mary style.

I dug around my gym bag and found a pair of my brother's sweat socks. I ran to the lady's room and reemerged as Dolly Parton Junior in less than two minutes flat. Get it? I tried to smooth out the lumps a bit, but it was quite obvious that I had stuffed my bra. Remember, I do nothing by half measures. Good or bad, I was committed to making that cheer squad.

When I returned to the field, I kept my arms crossed and waited. I watched as one classmate after another tumbled and jumped and cheered her heart out. Then it was my turn. I uncrossed my arms and ignored the wide-eyed looks of the coach and my fellow recruits. I cheered, I jumped, but as I arched my back to do the backflip, my right sweat sock wriggled out of place and crept its way out of my sleeve. By the time I did my simple tumble run, I was one sweat sock short of a pair. The coach said nothing, but my classmates were chuckling and whispering. My face was as red as a tomato, and my whole body was shaking, but pride would not allow me to acknowledge that stupid sweat sock on the ground. Needless to say, I hadn't conformed, and I did not make the team. The next day, some jokester left that sweat sock sitting on my desk at school, and I died a little.

That incident sealed my fate as a loser of the highest order. I had tried to conform, to be something I wasn't just so I'd be noticed, and I ended up spending the next several months making myself nearly invisible at school just to survive. I cried myself to sleep for weeks. Finally, my dad asked what was wrong. I had not given him or my mother the details of my failure. When I did, he started laughing so hard he almost fell off the sofa. I wanted to kill him in that moment. He finally took a breath and said, "That was a gutsy move kid. You committed to it and saw it through. I gotta give you that. But here's the thing—how about next time you just be you, do your best, and let God figure out the rest?" I informed him there would be no next time, and he simply said, "My daughter doesn't quit. I look forward to watching you cheer next fall." Dad walked out of the room leaving me sitting in a pile of self-pity and the horror that I might actually have to try out again.

When spring tryouts came, I was nervous but determined to redeem myself. I showed up, sans sweat socks, and cheered my heart out. The coaches actually cheered at the end of my audition. They *cheered*! My ability to hold two different people on my shoulders at the same time was the clincher. I made the squad for my seventh-grade year.

Ironically, all the things I hated about myself—my height, my freakish upper body strength, and my sturdy shoulders—were exactly what were needed on the team. No sweat socks required. Funny how God works. In order to be seen, all I had to do was be me.

Who knew?

Now here I was folding a different pair of sweat socks, trying to figure out how to fix an epic blunder that was so much worse than stuffing my bra in the sixth grade. I had hurt a friend deeply. I knew I had to ask for Miss J's forgiveness and at least try to make things better. So, the next day, I made muffins, wrote a letter of apology, and left them on her front steps. By midafternoon they reappeared on my front-porch steps, with the note torn in two and not one muffin eaten. It was over.

The funny thing about forgiveness is that you can ask for it, but the decision to grant it is up to the person who was hurt. Miss J and I never spoke again. That lesson has been etched deeply onto my heart, and I have never treated anyone in such a manner since then.

Comparison and Conformity

So how do these two incidents relate to each other? In both of them my desperation to be noticed led to disastrous outcomes. In both cases, I was humiliated as a result of my own choices. Feeling "less than" led me to conclude that I would be accepted only if I found a way to be "more than," no matter who I had to take down to do so. But what I really became was someone other than my true self, not at all the person God made me to be. These two events were catalysts for the change that made me able to accept God's unconditional love.

Did you see that? In order to accept God's love, I had to stop comparing myself to others, grasping for what I thought was needed, and truly receive what I had already been given. I had to let go of all the fear that drove me to conform and lean in to the truth of me.

What God Sees

God created each one of us in his image and likeness, but we often try to be someone other than who he made us to be. It's as if we see who we are and say to God, "Ummm actually, I'd like that gift or that talent. I want to be like Susie or Jane." God loves us all the time and just as we are. But we allow our self-perception to be based on how others see us or treat us. We don't experience the truth we read in Jeremiah 31:3: "With age-old love I have loved you."

Why are we so quick to listen to the whispers of despair and derision? Why is it so easy to give in to the lies the Deceiver whispers into our hearts? I think it's easier to believe all the negative things the world tells us about ourselves than it is to believe that God will love us no matter what. Our internal self-portrait is all askew and needs a serious readjustment. Most of us spend years looking at ourselves in a carnival funhouse mirror. (No, you really *don't* look like that!)

So how do we see the truth? It all begins with the relationship we have with the Father and the daily conversation known as prayer. I cannot know who I am unless I am listening directly to the Source. When we forget who we are, who God made us to be, we forget that he sees us with the eyes of a loving Father. We forget that when he looks at us, he sees not only what we are, but all we can be. He sees his beautiful, strong, talented child, made to do great things.

So stop thinking that you don't measure up, and don't listen to the lie that you need to be someone else in order to have a life filled with beauty and joy. Trust me, you don't need sweat socks. Instead, see your reflection in God's eyes, and know that who you are right now, in this moment, is awesome. You are made in the image and likeness of the King, who made you out of love and for love. Embrace the One who loves you and created you for a purpose and a reason, a mission only you can accomplish. God has great things in store for you, and he wants you exactly as you are.

CHAPTER 2

love Is the linchpin

⌬

I always wanted to be a mother. I never really thought about how hard it would be or the sacrifices motherhood would require of me. I just wanted someone to look at me with love and devotion, the way I used to look at my parents before adolescence.

I remember how excited I was the first time I held my son, Jonathan, in my arms. At twenty-two years old, I was confident in my diaper-changing ability and thought I knew just about everything there was to know about parenting him. After all, I grew up with six younger siblings and had been babysitting since I was thirteen. It wasn't *that* hard.

Then we brought him home, and within thirty-six hours I became terrified that we had just made the worst mistake of our lives. A baby doesn't do what you need them to do when you want them to do it. They have their own schedules, personalities, likes and dislikes, and very little patience or flexibility.

Jonathan was stubborn and very particular; thirty years later, he still is. In fact, he was colicky and required a lot of rocking and bouncing during that first year. But when he looked at me with that little toothless grin, I was happy. We made a pretty good team, my J-man and I—so good that Jerry and I decided to expand our little team. Our daughter, Courtney, was born almost three years later.

After being raised in a household with six brothers and only one sister, I was thrilled to have a girl. My future was *pink*! The clothes and the hair bows and the teeny-tiny Mary Jane shoes—everything had a ruffle butt, and it was spectacular. Of course, Courtney also had her own temperament, likes, and dislikes.

When Courtney was five weeks old, she began having unexplainable grand-mal seizures, and my version of motherhood was forever altered. At seven months, she had an allergic reaction to some medication we gave her to stop the seizures. As a result, she suffered severe brain damage, lost her sight, and never advanced beyond a developmental age of nine months in the twenty-two years we were able to love and care for her this side of heaven.

To say that our family was unprepared for this outcome would be an understatement of gargantuan proportion. We had no idea what to do, but we just kept moving, because if we stopped, we feared that the whole house would fall down, and no one would survive the collapse.

Judged from a Distance

One day at the playground Jonathan was running up and down the slide while I pushed Courtney around in her wheelchair. Another little family showed up but kept their distance across the playground. I didn't think anything of it at the time. Jonathan and I continued to enjoy the bright sunshine and beautiful spring day.

Then Courtney had a seizure. It was loud and scary, and at one point she held her breath and began to turn purple. This was not unusual, so I talked to her through it and blew gently in her face to encourage her to take a breath. Jonathan came over to her side, held her hand, and told her everything was going to be OK. Three minutes later I looked up and saw the other family just standing there staring at us, horrified at what they had just witnessed. I simply smiled, waved, and said, "She's okay."

That mom's reaction remains with me to this day. She gathered her little ones up and rushed them to the car, looking back toward us at least twice. No words were exchanged, just an expression of complete terror on her face. I gazed down at Jonathan and said it was time to go home; Courtney had had enough sunshine for the day. Jonathan's response tore me in two.

"Mama, why do people always run away from us? Don't they see that Courtney's just like them? Her brain is hurt, that's all." He leaned over to his sister, who was now sleeping, and whispered, "It's okay, Court. I see you. I won't run away." Then he took off running for one more slide down that slide, completely oblivious to my tears. Jonathan understood how to see Courtney as God saw her, perfect just as she was—as someone to love, not someone to fear.

Now let me be clear: Was I hurt? Yes. Was I mad at the woman for her reaction to a scary event she had no control over? Absolutely not. It was just a microcosm of what was happening more and more whenever we were out together. But my five-year-old spoke truth. People always ran when they didn't know what to do with our very unique family. Their lack of empathy and compassion tore at my heart every single time it happened. And I felt sorry for myself too. My motherhood looked different from everyone else's, and that was incredibly isolating. At the time, I had not even considered how hard it was for Jonathan. To be seen only to be rejected felt harsh and unfair.

As we walked back to the house, I remembered the first time I had met a different family. I wondered if they had ever experienced what we just had, realizing that without a doubt they must have. My heart hurt for them, but I smiled when I thought about the joy they brought to my life then and now. I didn't realize until right then that God had been preparing me for that day on the playground since the sixth grade.

Best Friends

I think it's been pretty well established that I was *not* a fan of school. Maybe it's because my dyslexia was undiagnosed until college. Maybe it's because my siblings were all athletically gifted and pretty brilliant, and I was not. Maybe it's because I hated to iron my Peter Pan collared shirts and box-pleated skirts every day. All I know is that school was never where I wanted to be.

Until I met Suzanne.

I don't remember the first time I met my childhood best friend, but I do know that from the sixth grade on we were inseparable. Suzanne was taller than I was (quite a feat at the age of eleven). She was kind, always smiling, and incredibly funny. Everyone loved Suzanne. Her laugh was infectious, and as a transfer student to my little grade school, she had a clean slate. She was gregarious and open-hearted while I was just plain awkward. She was smart, except in math, and both of us were placed into Mr. Sharp's remedial math class for middle school. While most of the school was learning algebra, we were just trying not to screw up long division.

We used to pass notes during class talking about which classmate we'd like to dance with at the eighth-grade dance, how cute the young assistant football coach was, or how much we wanted to get the math teacher his own case of Listerine because, man, did he have bad breath. Not much got by us in the social comings and goings of our grade school, and we found some way to laugh and joke about it all. Whenever I was with Suzanne, I was completely at ease and never felt the need to prove myself in any way. She even forgave me for the sweat-sock stunt and taught me to turn it into one hell of a story, the stuff of legends. She was so awesome that I even asked my mom if Suzy could be my sister in real life. Mom just chuckled and said she was happy I had *finally* found a friend. As much as that hurts to type, she wasn't wrong.

Suzanne was my *only* friend.

At school, the two of us were locked at the hip. We played on the Catholic Youth Organization basketball team together (she was the center, I was the forward), and we pulled the *best* eighth-grade prank our school had seen in years. I was even willing to take the fall to protect her, but that's a story for another time.

The first time I was invited to her house after school still is one of my favorite memories. First, she had a color TV. My family was *still* in black-and-white land—and yes, people, it was 1979. It just never seemed to be the right time to purchase one, or so said my father. Second, Suzanne was allowed to watch *General Hospital*, a very popular soap opera my mother called the "devil's tool." Third, there were always snacks. Always. Good snacks, like Doritos and Fritos, Peanut M&M's and real Ho Hos, not the Little Debbie imitations we had at my house.

The best part, though, was her brother, Jeff. He was funny, treated me like a rock star, and always greeted me with a hug and a smile. I was lucky if my brothers spoke to me, let alone smiled. (Just to be clear, we are grown-ups now and smile at one another and laugh together all the time. But in junior high, this was not the case.)

Now before you go and think that I had a crush on Jeff, I will just put it out there that, yes, I did. But probably not in the way you're thinking. Jeff had intellectual disabilities, which caused developmental delays, slurred speech, and other impediments. He loved Michael Jackson and would sing the lyrics to "Thriller" at the top of his lungs, and dang if he didn't know them all. One of my favorite memories was when he would sing Madonna's "Like a Virgin" in his deep male voice, cracking at the higher notes and then just busting out laughing when he came to the big finale. He was pure joy, and I loved being around him.

Every time we met, Jeff and I would have a sing-off, which he always won. He had a mind for math and computers, the things in which I struggled most. Jeff never had to do anything for his family to love him completely. He was just Jeff, and there was a freedom there I didn't know existed. He was valued for who he was, for the uniqueness of who God made him to be. I have to admit that I longed for what he had—including the joy, the color TV, and the really cool sister.

Suzanne didn't have many school friends over because she was very protective of Jeff. Very few were allowed into the inner circle, and the fact that her family welcomed me with open arms makes me want to cry even now. Mr. and Mrs. C are two of my favorite people on the planet, and I will never forget how they always smiled when they saw me at church or at school, in the neighborhood, or wherever. I was family to them and still am.

From here I can see how the time I spent with them prepared me for a life I didn't know was coming. They helped me to see the value of another person just as God created them to be, no adjustments needed. They taught me how to laugh at the awkward silences when others didn't know what to say and to embrace our individual uniqueness.

Transforming Love

Nothing in life is wasted, friend. God was using all of these experiences to help me navigate what I encountered with Jonathan and Courtney at that playground and for so many years afterward. Suzanne's family acted like they had won the lottery to have Jeff. We all have a mission, and one of Jeff's was to sing and laugh and make me fall in love with innocence and wonder.

As I walked home with my two very unique children that sunny afternoon, I hummed "Like a Virgin" and remembered Jeff. I quietly thanked him for preparing me to be Courtney's mother in a way he would never understand, one that changed the course of my life. I said a prayer for my sweet friend Suzanne and asked God to bless her wherever she was at that moment. Her gift of love and acceptance had ripple effects in my life for the next two decades and beyond.

Many years later, on the day of Courtney's funeral, I needed a safe place to land in the midst of all the people coming to honor my daughter. I looked across the church, and there was Suzanne, standing quietly in the back, tears streaming down her eyes, arms open wide. In his faithfulness, God afforded me shelter just when I needed it most. I walked into that safe space, and we just held each other and wept.

I pulled back and looked straight into her dark eyes and said, "Thank you. Thank you for teaching me how to see someone the world thinks is different, is 'less than,' as a pure gift. Thank you for being the first example I can remember of a person accepting someone with a disability into their heart and loving them right where they were. Thank you for teaching me to see with my heart first and my very judgmental eyes second. Thank you for being there to cheer me on as we tried our best to love and care for Courtney the way your family has cared for Jeff. Thank you for being a true friend, with me at my worst and still choosing to see my best in that moment. You, my friend, have been the face of Christ to me for most of my life, and I just need you to know how grateful I am for the gift of you."

She was dumbfounded. She stood quietly for a few moments before simply saying. "But you saw me first, friend. You never judged me or my family, especially Jeff. You welcomed me into your home and your heart, and it meant everything."

In the exchange of truly authentic friendship, we saw each other as God saw each of us. We'd been given unique gifts and talents to build the kingdom of God, and we didn't even know it. That's the beauty of God, friend. He shows up in the ordinary and infuses mercy and grace to create something extraordinary.

What Suzanne and Jeff, along with their awesome parents, brought to my life was a level of acceptance I had not known was possible. They saw my awkward humor, rough manners, and supremely loud laugh, as well as my less-than-spectacular math skills, and loved me right where I was. They never asked me to change in any way whatsoever. By loving me and cheering me on, I was able then to turn around and do the same for them.

God Sees Us with Love

I have been blessed to have other women come into my life and "see" me, but Suzy was the first. She helped me to understand that there was nothing "wrong" with me. She never insisted that I change myself to fit a certain narrative or playbook. Instead, she allowed me the freedom to be loud and awkward and sing '80s tunes with her hairbrush and gush over what I would wear on my wedding day. And she stood by my side when peers were mean and life was hard. She showed me kindness and compassion when I felt "less than" and offered forgiveness whenever I offended.

I imagine this is how God sees us, my friend.

How often do we say to ourselves, to God, and to anyone else who might be listening, *I am stupid*, or *ugly*, or *just plain useless*? How many times have we stood off to the side while everyone else was dancing, our hearts bleeding, waiting for someone, *anyone*, to see us and believe that we are worthy of that dance? Imagine God standing next to you in that moment. What would he say?

You are beautiful and kind and worthy of love.

You are strong and capable and smart.

You are my child, and I see you and you are mine.

Let me love you right where you are.

Let's dance; shall we, my dear?

It breaks God's heart when all we see are our failures and our sins. It breaks his heart when we speak harsh words to ourselves and others in order to hide the hurt in our lives. It breaks his heart when we look into the mirror and see ugliness and lack, when all he created was wonder and beauty.

I had to learn to see myself as God sees me—and, boy, did it take a whole lot of time and heartache to get there. I first had to learn to accept God's love just as I had accepted Suzanne's friendship. That took courage: courage that didn't come naturally to me, courage I didn't know I had inside, courage that pushed me forward into God's loving arms. And you know where I found that courage? In God himself.

CHAPTER 3

The Courage to Be Real

❧

God and I have not always communicated well. I know. Shocking, right? I kept him at arm's length, and he put me in the penalty box. I saw him only as judge and jury, yet he kept trying to convince me to turn my heart toward him. He pursued me even when I had the "Do Not Disturb" sign on the door to my heart. It's just that he expected too much, and I was not ready to give it.

Because in order to have a new life, you must forfeit your old one—and all your false ones.

One of the areas of great woundedness in my life is the fact that I have never thought of myself as smart. It goes back to grade school where I was put in the remedial reading group in the first grade. Then, later, I was put in the "special" math class. It didn't matter what I did; academic success was not in the cards for me. I know now it's because I had an undiagnosed learning disability, which led to low self-esteem and a serious lack of confidence.

That, in turn, caused me to grasp for what was not mine and hide my true self. I discovered my learning disability while testing to be a reading tutor in college. Here I was trying to help someone else, and I was the one that needed help. Ironic, right? But instead of thinking, *Wow, Mary, you got through twelve years of school fighting an internal battle you couldn't even name,* I concluded that I was damaged and stupid. Those two lies are hard to shake.

I was afraid that I would never be good enough. So, to protect my heart and fragile ego, I never fully allowed others to see the truth of *me*. Instead, I hid behind different pretenses throughout my life. I tried to be someone else— someone who was smarter, funnier, and more worthy of love.

Writing It Down

I was in the third grade when I finally learned how to read. Once reading was unlocked, my life got so much richer and far less lonely. But while I could read the words, I didn't understand them, and they kept switching places on the page. One way I could keep the words from "swimming" was to write them down. This is how my love affair with the written word began.

I wrote down everything and am a copious notetaker to this day. It's how I comprehend what's important. Writing calms me down and makes everything manageable. That's why I kept a daily diary from an early age and also why I continued to write throughout my adult life. It was something that had nothing to do with any other part of my life. It wasn't about Jerry or the kids; it was mine and mine alone, and I cherished that. Within the pages of that journal, I was most honest with myself and with God, and I shared my heart in a way I did with no one else except my husband. In time I built up the courage to step out of hiding and share my words with a greater audience.

I dreamed of my first sweet inspirational romance novel on the shelves of Borders or Barnes & Noble, winning accolades and literary awards. It was going to be a beautiful romance, funny and light and sprinkled with a little Jesus. So I joined a local chapter of a professional writing group called the Romance Writers of America.

I was thrilled to be a part of something that had nothing to do with parenting or being a special-needs caregiver. It was completely separate from the many struggles I was facing at home and in my marriage at the time. This was all about seeing my name on a book cover one day, sharing a little bit of my heart, and finally being known for accomplishing something in the world.

One of the perks of the group is that you can also join a critique group. These handfuls of like-minded writers met weekly to brainstorm, go over one another's work, and help one another on the path to publication. I'd meet Sharon, Christine, Stephanie, and Karen at the local Barnes & Noble, review pages, brainstorm plot twists, and chat about what publishing houses or agents we planned to query. We dreamed of the *big* life that came with being an author. Each week, I'd bring my pages and sit through the critique. One at a time, the women would begin with something positive and then gently pick my writing apart, urging me on to excellence.

In the beginning, I loved my critique group. Over time, though, I began to feel uber-vulnerable and became resistant to the well-intended and constructive criticism. I had worked hard to get words on the page, so for someone to say they weren't my best work hurt. Every time the comments came, it was another reminder that I wasn't smart enough to write a book, no matter my effort. My fragile ego was out of control, but as I walked through the fog of confusion, I never once stopped and asked God for an assist. I relied completely on myself and just kept moving, afraid that if I stopped, I would never start again.

After a particularly brutal critique, I stopped submitting my work. I felt too vulnerable when my words were on the table, and I could no longer hide myself behind my words. Although my critique partners were trying their best to help me, I was unable to listen. I was not coachable.

I continued to attend my critique group for social support—it was one of my only chances to leave the house alone due to Courtney's need for care—and slowly the dynamic changed. These women became part of my inner circle. Yet, as much as I trusted them with my heart, it was still too hard to share the words. As time went on, they continued to call me out and encourage me to submit. They knew how afraid I was to share, so they kept a seat at the table just for me—the nonwriter in a writer's group.

In this group, I'd discovered how it felt to be accepted as smart and capable, creative and funny. And then, because I couldn't control the narrative, I lost it. My lack of humility got in the way of my creativity, and I was in for a bit of pruning. I'd found some success, but then, because I'd attached my identity to my words, I feared I was not enough.

Yet again, I was living through a case of déjà vu.

A Better Version of Us

When I was growing up, my family was very complicated. My father was a functioning alcoholic, and I was nineteen years old when he had his own "come to Jesus" experience that changed his life, and our family's, for the better. But before then, there was a lot of hiding and making excuses for certain behavior, especially when he was drinking. My dad had his own demons to fight, and it wasn't until he began to share his struggles with us as adults that we were able to understand and forgive him for things said and done.

When I was a sophomore in high school, my mom got sick. She had a tumor in her throat that needed to be removed surgically. It was a scary time, and because I was the oldest daughter, I was expected to step in and help my mom during her recovery. That meant taking over the domestic chores I despised such as cleaning the bathrooms, scrubbing the kitchen floor, and doing the laundry. I would have been happy all day long in the kitchen, but Dad said the ladies of the Church Sodality would be bringing meals, so I didn't need to worry about it. The most important thing was that the house was clean and respectable when they came to deliver the meals.

My mother kept a very clean home, but my dad was a pack rat. There were bookshelves upon bookshelves filled with all kinds of literature and law books. Every table and end table had a stack of something on it, paintings hung on the walls wherever you turned, and knickknacks were everywhere. My dad loved it that way. If it had been up to my mother, the aesthetic would have been quite different. Minimalim is her love language.

To be told that perfect strangers were coming was enough to send me into a panic of the highest order. I cleaned for two days before they came, and when I say "cleaned," I mean I hid everything I could—after all, that's what fifteen-year-olds do. There were books in the closet and under the sofa. There were piles carefully labeled with spiral notebook paper then carried downstairs, so when the people left, we could put them back and Dad would know where everything was. It was a game of hide-and-seek with clutter.

I made it my job to make sure there was no reason for anyone to judge me or my parents. We were already known as "that family" in so many circles—too many kids, too much noise—and I didn't want to add to the legend and lore. Besides, there was nothing I could do about the groovy orange-and-brown plaid sofa that dominated the living room. I just prayed no one would want to sit down, because they might find the plywood base was less than comfortable. You could thank my brothers for that jewel. They had jumped with a little too much zeal playing paratroopers and broken the base of the sofa. There wasn't much my dad couldn't fix with a sturdy piece of plywood and duct tape.

The message I got loud and clear was that we couldn't just be us; we had to be a *better version* of us. So, I scrubbed those sofa cushions, mopped the floors, and wiped down the walls as if the Queen of England herself was coming. After cleaning up the dishes and getting my younger siblings to bed, I spent the next several hours dusting and vacuuming and scrubbing again. There was no way to remove some of the signs and symbols of life from the walls or the floor, so I moved furniture around to hide what I could and scrubbed the rest until I just gave up. Mom was still in the hospital, so I was largely in charge along with my older brother, Chris. His job was all things outside. We were determined to make a good impression and make our parents proud of us.

Mrs. K brought the first meal. She was a neighbor known for her fried chicken and frosted sugar cookies. That night she brought both. I felt like Sally Field receiving her Oscar: "You like me, you really like me." The house was shining and still smelled like lemon Pledge. The floors gleamed, and I had already set the table using the "fancy" plates Mom had found on sale. Mrs. K helped me place the trays of food on the table and said, "Your family is quite a lot to feed. Your mother must be exhausted. You need to do more, Mary Beth. This house could use a good cleaning, and your mom will need your help."

My mouth opened and closed like a fish. *What? What did she just say? Are you freaking kidding me? Do more?* I had been busting my hump for two days so this chick could spend five minutes telling me we were "alot," and what I had done wasn't enough. I was hurt and angry, but all I could think to do in that moment was hide behind a huge smile and say, "I'll do my best, Mrs. K." Her response: "You need to do better than that." And with that, she smiled and left. Good thing there was Confession that week because I certainly brought down fire and brimstone in my head.

Didn't she see how hard I had tried? I had given it my very best effort. Did she just not care that I had gone above and beyond? And yet it still wasn't enough.

That night I went to bed and had a heart-to-heart with God. *When will I be good enough, God? When will I be able to just be me and stop hiding my broken heart behind*

*a smile? When does the love and acceptance come? When
is anyone going to know who I really am and be okay with
that?*

I got up and wrote it all down in my diary. I poured
out my anger and embarrassment and shared how worried I was about my mother. At the time, her future was
still unknown. I wrote about how irritated I was that my
younger siblings didn't do what I had asked them to do and
how flipping annoying it all was. In the pages of my diary,
I was raw and honest; there was no hiding in those words,
no shoving anything under the sofa. When I was finished,
I closed the book and went to bed knowing at least God
knew how hard I had tried.

The next day, however, nothing changed. There was no
"You're awesome" or "Thanks for doing such a great job"
from Dad. He was too distracted with Mom, so there was
just another "Get it done" as he went out the door to bring
my mom home. On top of that, Dad asked me to write a
thank-you note to Mrs. K and deliver it when I returned
her clean dishes.

All I wanted to do was spit on the pretty thank-you
card with a butterfly on the front that Dad had brought
at the People's Drug Store. Instead, I did what I had to
do and hid my feelings behind big swirling handwriting
and happy smiley faces. I did what Dad asked of me and
dropped it all off that afternoon.

What does any of this have to do with authenticity?

I had learned to hide. It was clear that neither I nor
my family measured up to the standards of acceptability
or perfection. I was told time and time again that we were
a burden and "too much." And that's how I had felt in my
writing critique group. My words were "too much."

Controlling the Narrative

Instead of relegating me to the coffeemaker and muffin-runs, Sharon, Christine, Stephanie, and Karen knew I was capable of more and urged me on. But still I struggled. My need to control how others perceived my work prevented me from seeing the truth: they were gently trying to help me.

The funny thing is that even though I opted not to work on a book, I started writing a blog. There, I began to share about my daily life with Courtney and gave others a glimpse into what it was like to care for a severely disabled child. In 2007, no one else was doing that online. It was exciting and new, and my critique partners supported me all the way.

I was comfortable with blogging because I had complete control of the narrative. I could create whatever world I wanted and give my readers as much or as little information about myself and my life as I desired. And I could tweak the truth for dramatic effect because I controlled the flow of information. So, I presented our life with joy, setting aside the harder parts that weren't so clean and happy. Readers commented on the confidence I expressed as Courtney's mother and in my role as her caregiver. The wonderful thing was that I could do that without anyone knowing the inner workings of my heart. They didn't know that I cried every day or that I was still grieving the loss of the life I thought I would have with my child. They didn't know about the daily challenges in my marriage or how my son was struggling. They saw only that I was happy and had my you-know-what together. And I clung to that false image for months and months.

At the same time I was showing up for critique group, I was also attending a weekly women's prayer group. We were all in different seasons of life but were brought together by faith and a desire to grow in holiness. We came together every Thursday and laid out our lives before one another and asked for wisdom and guidance. They too met me where I was and asked nothing more of me. Still, even in that sacred circle I was afraid to open my heart fully and completely. Again, I shared what I was comfortable with and hid the rest inside.

Until one day those two worlds collided, and I was called out for my lack of authenticity.

My friend Cathy C. knew me and my true heart well. We had been praying side by side every week for a few years, and she understood the depth of my brokenness. She'd also seen how strained and stressful my life truly was.

When Cathy called me one afternoon to chat, her first question hit me in the heart. "You know I love you, right?"

Whenever I hear that I know correction is coming. I was right.

She continued, "Why are you sounding like a Holy Hannah on your blog when I know you cuss? Why are you preaching to people instead of exposing the ugly underside of your life? Why aren't you letting people know who you really are?"

I was stunned. I desperately wanted the world to know me as a woman of faith, one of deep holiness without the ugliness of doubt and derision. Words were life to me. I had finally had the courage to share them publicly, and now they were being blown back in my face. At least that's how I felt in the beginning of the conversation. Then the Holy Spirit showed up and the tide turned. I was able to receive what Cathy C. had to say, and for the first time the correction stung but didn't defeat me.

As the conversation continued, Cathy C. poured wisdom and grace into my heart. We were sisters in Christ, and because of that bond, I was able not only to hear but also to really listen to and receive her words. She knew my hesitation to be completely honest and open. She also knew some of my past pain and clearly understood how it was holding me back from stepping into the truth. We prayed together on the phone that day, and by the time I hung up, I felt the change coming. I was scared but dug deep into prayer.

After thinking and praying long and hard about what Cathy C. said, I realized that I wasn't confident enough to share any part of my life with complete authenticity. I was convinced that if I shared the truth, if I revealed my brokenness, then judgment and rejection would follow. I was terrified that if I told the world how hard my life truly was, about how much I struggled to find joy and be positive, people would run away in fear. Because honestly, at that point in my life, if given a choice, I would have run away too.

On my counterfeit blog, I was a hero. I was strong and intelligent, talented and long-suffering. And why not? Why would I want the world to see the troubled, confused, scared, and angry Mary? Why would I want the world to see all my brokenness and fear, my lack of self-confidence as a wife and mother, as a woman of faith? I couldn't handle being known as someone other than the woman I had created in my own head.

As a result, I'd become *un*known.

Embracing the Truth

That conversation with Cathy changed everything. The following week I asked my critique group for their advice on how to move forward. Fear controlled every key on my laptop. Sharon, Christine, Stephanie, and Karen knew this truth as well, but instead of challenging me, they supported me. They wanted the world to know me as they did: a sassy, bold, funny, creative, over-the-top woman who loved nothing more than baking a dozen cupcakes for a friend in need of some encouragement and love. To them, I was the woman in the kitchen surrounded by friends as we prepared a meal together; a friend sitting and holding a friend's hands as we asked God for healing and grace; a woman whose wisdom, mercy, and empathy were just as real as her brokenness.

So, I took a chance and began to write the whole, unvarnished truth. I shared my hurt as well as my heart and my fear along with my faith. I put both my wisdom and my wackiness out there and even cussed in a blog post. And people came to know the true me. Because my friends were able to speak truth in love, because they knew me and loved me as I was, they were able to draw me out of hiding and into the light of authenticity. And you know what happened? I ended up with a blog that got thousands of hits per day—a huge deal during the early internet.

And because I had finally found the courage to be my true self, I was able to walk through some really hard healing. But more importantly, being honest about the joys and sorrows of raising a severely disabled child and my own internal struggles was helpful to others. Perfect strangers started to reach out to me and say, "I thought I was the only one who felt like a perfect failure or that I'm not doing enough." It was an eye-opening moment for me.

I had always struggled with words, to read and understand as well as to have them read and be understood. But God uses every experience, friend, every single one. I could never have known that over the course of my lifetime God would use what I perceived as my greatest weakness to bring forth his greatest redemption in my life—all through the power of words. What I needed to do was let go of my pride, own my brokenness, banish my feelings of inadequacy, and step into the mission that God was still revealing to me. When I stopped trying to be someone else, I began to discover that although I wasn't perfect, I wasn't the lies I had been telling myself for decades either.

A New Bathing Suit

When hiding looks like the best option, it's good to remember that we cannot hide from God. He knows us and loves us just as we are, flaws and all. To me, this is like shopping for a new bathing suit. Yes. You read that correctly: the horror known as the how-will-I-possibly-be-able-to-look-at-myself-in-the-mirror-with-all-the-things-that-are-wrong-with-my-body-but-I-need-to-buy-a-bathing-suit-for-our-family-vacation experience. Most women dread this more than getting on the scale at the doctor's office for the yearly weigh-in.

It's the thing nightmares are made of.

You can stop screaming now. No, seriously, stop. My ears are bleeding.

I spend what feels like five days looking for just the right bathing suit. I've got the black bathing suit with the tummy control panel and the shirred sides that will assist in hiding that postpartum belly. Forget the fact that my youngest child was born more than two decades ago, and I look like I gave birth last week.

Next up is a fabulously fun suit with wider straps and a swim skirt that reminds me of pictures of my grandmother from the 1920s family photo album. And then there's yet another one-piece with stripes going vertically because I know, without a doubt, that vertical stripes make everything better.

But first I'm going to try on the tankini. I am immediately transported to the beaches of Florida during my senior-year high school trip with the marching band. The trip where I decided a tan was a must for prom. The trip where I used baby oil instead of sunscreen and, after one day, my Irish skin protested with a riotous case of sun poisoning accompanied by second-degree burns on my shoulders.

That didn't happen to you? Just me? Gotcha. Moving on.

I strip down and see everything—every little bump and curve, the ones that are supposed to be there and new ones I've never seen before. I tug the top over my head, and I feel like a four-year-old putting on a wetsuit. I'm stuck with my arms in the air, underwear on the bottom, completely exposed, flailing around the room. I finally get the top pulled down and yank on the bottoms. There is a gap between the pieces. *I don't think so*. Once I decide no one needs to know that much about me, I move on.

The one-piece with the vertical stripes is next. Surely the vertical lines will make me look taller and thinner. Vertical stripes trick the eye into thinking those extra five pounds, plus the added ten caused by stress eating, don't matter. Unfortunately, those vertical stripes I thought would deflect do the opposite. I now feel like a circus tent. It takes another ten minutes to peel that tent off, and I kick it across the dressing-room floor. Then I stomp on it. Thank goodness no one but me will ever see that sight. No one needs to see the truth: my shame, my sin, my bad choices made after midnight standing in front of the fridge.

I reach for the black one with the tummy control panel and know within thirty seconds it's not going to go on. It's more like a sausage casing than a bathing suit. How did it come to this? This cannot be my life. I talk to myself in the mirror, "You are a stupid fat girl. You will be laughed off that beach before lunchtime." This is just the beginning of the inner conversation I have with myself, and it's getting uglier by the minute.

I'm down to the last try-on.

It's a retro suit and covers all the right places without revealing too much. It's flattering with its simple cut and bright color. It feels safe and right. Not too bold, not too much. I'm plenty without my swimsuit shouting to everyone around me.

I stand there for what feels like hours, and I look at myself in that suit from every angle. One moment I think, *This is it. This will work. It's flattering as much as dressing a cake pop can be flattering, and it covers what needs to be covered.* With its bright color and simple lines, though, I know I will still stand out on the beach. People will know that I enjoy baking and do not exercise as I should. They will know that I have put myself last in the list for decades, and in the next breath all kinds of hateful things fill my mind and my inner calm is gone.

I take the swimsuit off, and I walk away. I am not willing to take any risk to be known that intimately.

And so for the next two summers I went without a swimsuit because to be seen and known was too much to bear. Right behind the fear was self-hatred and envy of all those skinny women who could control themselves around a chocolate cupcake while I could not.

Easier to Hide

The photos I have from that time tell the story of a woman who was not at ease with herself in any way. In those photos, I'm always in shorts and a T-shirt while my husband and children are in swimsuits. I was not brave enough to be myself, because I believed that if people knew me, really knew me, they would walk away. I felt completely set apart from everyone else, and, believe it or not, I was okay with the separation at the time. It was a better option than being rejected. I hid in those shorts and T-shirts and half-lived by my own choice.

For those two years, we lived ten minutes from the beach and went only four times while we lived there. I built a cage around my heart to protect myself from the judgment of others. I had no desire to be known by anyone, including God. The funny thing is, God already knew my inner pain and struggles. He was present for all of my internal drama. If I'd just trusted him, things would've been different. But God and I were not in that place yet. I found it easier to hide, and so I did—until I couldn't hide anymore.

I had to let go of the distorted view I had of myself and allow my heart to be known by the One who has known me from the beginning of time. I had to stop trying to hide behind some other persona that was not my authentic self and allow the world to see me as I was. It was time to get back to that dressing room and try again. The beach was calling my name, and there were sandcastles to be built and waves to jump. It was time to face the mirror and know I was beautiful and strong, kind and smart, a child of the Most High King ready to receive her inheritance of love.

You too are a daughter of the King, created in his image and likeness, made for a mission that is yours and yours alone. I'm guessing that sometimes your brokenness keeps you from jumping in with both feet. Be bold anyway. You have everything you need within you to complete this mission. You just have to believe it and then find the courage to act on it. Stop hiding and start listening to the still, small voice of your Creator, who is calling you to holiness, calling you to be yourself, calling you to be the daughter he made you to be and to serve in his name for his glory.

CHAPTER 4

The Courage to Surrender

G od knew what he was doing when he created you and me. He equipped each of us with unique gifts and talents so that we could accomplish the mission he has for us. We are one-of-a-kind puzzle pieces made to fit together to create a masterpiece. As much as I knew that truth in my head, though, it took decades for it to travel to my heart.

God gifted me with the charisms of wisdom, mercy, and hospitality to encourage people, not to write a romance novel. He knew that my heart needed to invest hope in others, because by doing so, I could cling to hope in a new way. He knew that it could be done through my words—both written and spoken. I just had to have the courage to know and believe in myself as he knew and believed in me to have the confidence and faith to speak and write. So while I wasted time looking for perfection, God was looking for surrender.

Words gave me both life and purpose. I dug deeper into blogging, encouraging other moms with special-needs kids to find hope and joy in their challenging journeys. I simply "spoke" to the page and allowed the Holy Spirit to work through that. No editing or overthinking went into my posts. I just shared my heart and my horrible grammar, and before I knew it there was a community of people showing up, praying for me and my family, and encouraging me to keep risking the vulnerability required to speak the truth and share my heart. Because I had finally let go of who I thought I needed to be in order to be accepted, I was able to make my way along the path of self-discovery to a place of healing and wholeness.

I had finally stopped striving for what others had and started to dig deep into what God had for me. For seven years I poured my heart out through the written word several times a week. I wrote about doctor visits and hospital stays that challenged my sanity. I wrote about Courtney's shenanigans, like the time she started hootin' and hollerin' when I bent over at school and split my pants. Courtney was blind. So how she knew to laugh at that exact moment is known only to her and God. It really wasn't that funny. I wrote about how the little old ladies at church were always fussing over her and how she would just preen with the extra attention. And I wrote about the time her brother got into a fight with a schoolmate because they called her retarded. I surrendered my pride about how it would make me look and shared it all.

I answered emails from perfect strangers who felt safe enough to share their deepest wounds, knowing I wouldn't judge them in their struggle. I became known for my words and for being Courtney's mom, caring for her daily needs while wearing a fabulous pair of statement earrings paired with the perfect apron, all while holding an award-winning Apple Crumble Pie. That was on Tuesdays. On Wednesdays it was a stained T-shirt with yoga pants and no makeup. It wasn't perfect; it was real.

Swallowed Whole

Then my whole world turned on its axis. On December 27, 2014, at 1:51 a.m., my beautiful daughter, Courtney Elizabeth Lenaburg, took her last breath this side of heaven. I was swallowed whole by the devastating, heart-breaking, soul-sucking darkness known as grief, and I thought I would never again see the light. All the encouragement I had given others to do the hard things and fight the good fight fell short and felt insincere. I wanted nothing to do with anything positive or happy. My motherhood and my craft of writing both seemed completely inadequate and inconsequential in the face of grief.

So, I stopped writing. I stopped living. I stopped caring. I wallowed in that pool of grief like it was my job and I had just gotten a promotion and a raise. God, however, had different plans. Those people who had come alongside my family and me in those years of blogging did not stop caring. They prayed. They sent letters of consolation and hope. They showed up at the door with flowers and meals and hugs; and over the course of the next few months, I slowly made my way back to the light and began to write again.

Writing became a love letter to my daughter. I needed to write down the legacy of beauty she had left behind. The written word was once more an oasis where I could pour

my heart out onto the page, believing that God already
knew the laments before I could put them to paper. To
be known by a loving and gracious God in that moment
brought me a peace I had never experienced. In time, it
also allowed me to know others and walk with them in
their journeys of grief, suffering, and pain.

Still a Mom

My first clear memory after Courtney died was our parish high school youth ministry winter retreat in Febru-
ary. I remember Eucharistic Adoration that weekend.
Surrounded by one hundred high schoolers who were so
open to the Holy Spirit, to me it felt as if the room had
an actual heartbeat. I was agitated and ill at ease. I was so
overwhelmed by God's presence that I quietly wept in the
back of the room. I felt lost as to what to do. My job was
to intercede for the kids in prayer and comfort any who
were struggling. I wasn't sure if I could be any help to the
teens that night because I still needed comforting so badly
myself. Taking a deep breath, I opened my arms in praise
and worship as we sang with one voice, and gave the night
to God. I was tired of trying to hold it all. I couldn't do it.
He would have to step up.

Suddenly, I felt my heart break open. I bowed my head
and asked the Lord to heal the hurt and show me where
he wanted me to go now. I thanked him for the gift of my
daughter's life and for how he had shown us how to live
with so much trust and hope while loving her. But I was
confused and struggling with my purpose. I had spent two
decades caring for our special-needs daughter, and my
identity had been wrapped up in being her mother and

caregiver. I had been "Courtney's mom" for so long that no one called me Mary anymore. I didn't recognize my life (or myself) without her. If I was meant to move, God would need to move me.

I raised my eyes to see the monstrance in front of me. God was right there, looking straight into my heart. He *knew* my pain, and he loved me profoundly. I understood in that moment that I was his daughter, fully covered by the mantle of his protection and provision, so I cried out to my heavenly Father for restoration and direction.

"Please, Father, show me. Show me all of this was for something," I whispered through my tears. "Show me how to go on. What do you want from me?"

There was a young man quietly crying on the step in front of me, also overwhelmed at that moment. I watched him for a while, then felt called to go and offer him a tissue and my presence. That's it. As I sat there gazing prayerfully at the Lord and interceding for this young man, I felt my Courtney's presence so strongly and heard her whisper into my heart, "You will always be my mom. Love them like you loved me. That's all you need to do."

In that moment I understood that God was asking me to once again surrender my future to him. This time came easier than the last. I took a deep breath and smiled for the first time since her death. God was not calling me to a *different* mission; he was calling me to a *deeper* mission. I was still a mom, still called to love and serve and encourage. I was just going to be doing it for others.

As I sat there, the young man put his head on my shoulder and whispered, "Thanks, Mama Mary. God knew I needed my mom, and he sent me you." We sat in silence for a bit before there was another teen who needed similar attention. That same scene was repeated over and over that night.

God *knew* my heart, and he was going to lead the way. I just had to surrender my grief and expectations and follow him.

That night, God showed me that I could continue to love as a mother even though my child was dead. He called me to trust him with his gift of motherhood, so that I could fully enter into the mission field he had prepared for me. There was peace—so much peace to be seen and known and loved in the midst of my darkest hour. I had felt that peace before, and as my mind struggled to remember, tears spilled over. I kept my eyes on him, simply receiving what he wanted to give me in that moment. "Your plan and not mine," I prayed from the depths of my heart.

There was no hiding in that meeting of hearts. God knew every hair on my head and every sin in my life. He knew every bad choice made in pride, and he understood all my pain. Grief cannot be hidden. It spills over the edges of life and touches everything. It clarifies and makes priorities clear. I had spent so many years trying to control how people saw me, trying to hide the parts that were less than desirable. My daughter, Courtney, couldn't do that. She simply was who she was. And she was loved abundantly. I needed to be like Courtney: open, free, and simply me. I needed to stop fighting and start listening and leaning in.

So how was I able to surrender to God's unconditional love then, when I had rejected it so many times before due to my false humility and lack of trust? First, I had to fully understand what love was, both conditional and unconditional, and how it looked and felt in my life. Then I had to experience love both in real time and in the real world.

That process took me back to high school and my first pair of designer jeans.

Yes. Jeans.

Wait! Aren't we in the middle of adoration with a sea of high schoolers? We're talking about Jesus, not jeans. Yes—but stay with me here. There is a point.

Let me tell you how I confused physical love with the overwhelming love of Jesus and how he brought me back to him.

The Right Pair of Jeans

You know that feeling of fierce confidence that comes over you when you have found just the right pair of jeans? You feel powerful, as if you could rule the world or at least impress that boy you liked in chemistry class.

Do jeans equal love?

When I was in high school, jeans told you something about the girl who was wearing them. You had Levi's, which were what every mother in America wore and no teenager would be caught dead in. You had Gloria Vanderbilt jeans, which said, "I'm classy and sophisticated," a worth-more-than-a-milkshake-and-a-large-fries-on-a-Friday-night-date kind of gal. In other words, someone who required a sit-down dinner, nothing too fancy, but just fancy enough to require the dressy top and high-heeled shoes, along with those Vanderbilt jeans. I was not a fancy gal and felt like an imposter in those jeans, and I was totally okay with the milkshake and fries, because honestly, I didn't think I was good enough for the sit-down meal.

Then there were the Jordache jeans. These were for the flashy girls, the cheerleaders, and the Pom Squad girls—the ones who dated the high school quarterback. Oh, how desperately I wanted to be a Jordache girl, but they never quite fit. The low waistband and thick embroidery on the back pockets that drew the eye to your bum—well, there was nothing to see there. Especially on me. Flat as an ironing board.

Guess jeans were for rich girls. I used to dream of buying a pair of Guess jeans, but one pair would have required an entire month's babysitting money. I would head to the mall on a Friday night with girlfriends, and we would try on pair after pair just to feel like we were somebody. The VJs on MTV wore Guess jeans. So did the girls whose families belonged to the country club where I bussed tables. I lived on the wrong side of the tracks for Guess jeans.

My jeans of choice were Calvin Kleins. Brooke Shields was plastered across every billboard in town wearing her Calvins, and who didn't want to be loved like Brooke? She was feisty and beautiful, sexy in an innocent sort of way, and very confident. She was everything I wanted to be. Not too flashy, but just enough. Classy without being stuffy. Attractive without being in your face. Besides, what did I know about the power or responsibility of my femininity in high school? I just knew that when I wore Calvins, I was the bomb. I worked two jobs and saved for two months to buy my first pair of Calvin Kleins on sale at Lord & Taylor. I was now worthy of love.

What kind of love? I had no clue, but I did know that wearing those jeans would make me visible, and that was all I cared about. Love equaled attention, and attention equaled worth. It was so backward in my head and even worse in my heart.

In college, my need for love, both physical and emotional, nearly destroyed my life. All I cared about was my social life. I was tired of being set aside as not smart enough or pretty enough or cool enough. So, once again, I started chasing after what I thought love was. I wore my Calvin Kleins a size too small and flirted at every opportunity. If there was a party and I wasn't working, I was there. I made out with a guy in my psych class, and I pretty much stalked one of my former high school crushes. I worked that '80s Madonna hair and the funky clothes from the Bangles music videos. The amount of hair spray and blue eye shadow I used would have bankrupted Barnum & Bailey Circus.

I was on a mission to be loved, and this time I would not fail.

One Friday night, my friend Kim invited me to go DC barhopping. (The drinking age at the time was eighteen, so nothing illegal was happening.) She wanted to go dancing and knew the perfect place. That night things changed for me forever.

Loud music, crowded dance floor, guys asking me to dance and complimenting my outfit. As the drinks flowed, I reveled in all the attention, until one of my dance partners propositioned me. He actually thought I was a prostitute looking for my evening's mark. I was shocked and humiliated and tried to laugh my way out of the situation, trying to avoid causing a scene. I excused myself to go to the lady's room, and I quietly grabbed my friend Kim to accompany me. I was in full panic mode. This was definitely *not* the love I was looking for.

I relayed what was happening, and Kim led me to the back exit. Unfortunately for us, that gentleman and his friend noticed and chased us as we ran down the street to get to our car. I can still hear the insults and slurs they hurled at us. In that moment my guardian angel sent a police officer who stopped them and prevented them from further pursuit. As the fear and panic dissipated, shame began to sink in and settle in my bones.

Once more, I was proven unworthy of love. I had grasped for something that was outside of the rules and failed again. And this time, it almost cost me something very precious, my innocence and virginity.

The next morning, I found myself in Mass apologizing to God for my horrid behavior and asking him to forgive me. I told God I was done. I was never going to walk into a bar again or stalk anyone or pursue this elusive thing called love. If he was God, then he could fix it. But he would have to bring the right person to me. Until then, I was going to focus on getting my life in order and becoming a better person.

Love That Fits

As I looked up during the moment of consecration, once again face-to-face with God, I heard a voice say, "I love you. You are mine." I knew immediately that I had heard Jesus. Tears fell as I kept apologizing for being such a weak and sinful human. He simply answered, "Enough. Just let me love you." As I received him in Holy Communion that day, I accepted that love, truly accepted it into my very being. I finally felt an odd and unfamiliar peace, one that left my constantly planning and plotting mind confused. I knew God had heard my apologies and my promise and that I didn't have to do a thing; he would take care of me.

I left that church that morning feeling loved and cared for in a way I had never previously experienced. God would answer the greatest desire of my heart, and love would come—first from him, and then from the one he chose for me.

I went about my life differently after that. I got rid of the Calvin Kleins and chose the safe and serviceable Levi's. I stopped wearing blue eye shadow and teasing my hair, worked to build authentic friendships with people, and spent more time with my family. I didn't date or attend parties and opted for an ordinary life, hidden and quiet instead. I surrendered my old life in hopes of building this one.

Three months to the day after that Mass, I found myself being dragged to Annapolis, Maryland, so my friend Kim could see her new boyfriend. You don't say no to a girlfriend in love. She needed someone to drive with her, so I and our mutual friend Christine piled in the 1970 Chrysler LeBaron and headed toward the US Naval Academy. Kim and her boyfriend had set Christine and me up with blind dates so it wouldn't be too awkward. I shook my head and expressed my displeasure. I felt like the house mother from every '80s sorority film I had ever seen. I was there to encourage and support. That was it.

That night, my blind date stood me up—further proof that God would provide for me at the right time and place. Christine's blind date, however, did show up, and he was a real gem. Jerry was funny, articulate, kind, respectful, and super handsome in his dress blues. He did his best to make sure we both danced and felt welcome. He was the polar opposite of the guy in that DC bar.

Eventually another midshipman joined us and made googly eyes at Christine. Since she was officially Jerry's date, he quietly pulled Jerry aside to ask his permission to dance with her. Jerry left it to Christine's discretion, giving her full freedom to choose and respecting her comfort level as any true gentleman would. They went off to dance, leaving Jerry and me to get to know each other better. No pressure, no shenanigans, just laughter and bad dance moves.

We parted ways that night with the promise to stay in touch.

One week later, I found myself back in Annapolis on my first official date with Jerry: attending Mass and then brunch. As I knelt for the consecration, I looked up at the altar and saw us standing there, dressed in white, exchanging vows. Jesus was standing with us, our hands in his, his face beaming. He said, "I love you. Now let me love you through him." Not exactly what I'd expected to happen on a first date, but once again, I had a feeling of deep peace come over me. At that moment, Jerry took my hand. I looked at him and smiled. He winked at me and tucked my hand securely in his arm. I could feel his heart beating. I took a deep breath and thanked God for loving me so well.

For the first time in my life, I had been patient. I had not grasped for attention and had waited for God to direct my path. Now, here I was looking up into the face of the man I would eventually marry. I wish I could say that the next two years were filled with only grace and beauty, but that would be a lie.

God had answered my prayer so directly, yet I eventually stopped waiting and started grasping again. I started to look at Jerry as the answer to my loneliness instead of as my path to holiness. It was like I had amnesia. I struggled to remain in that head-and-heart space of abiding because grasping came so easily to me. "Doubt" was my middle name, and I never felt strong enough to completely close that door. And doubt felt a lot like Calvin Klein jeans to me, too tight and constricting, squeezing out hope and faith as I tried to zip them up.

A Future Filled with Hope

I remembered that first-date Mass as I sat in that room filled with teens seeking hope and love and receiving God's mercy and grace. I remembered that young woman who would grasp instead of receiving and resolved not to go back there again.

The peace God had for me was mine to pick up or lay down. I was done with not being enough. I was done with holding on to the past and all the doubt it brought with it.

I was finally ready to receive the future God had for me.

After that weekend things felt lighter. The grief was still very present, but I could breathe again. I could see a future filled with hope once more. I knew time would help ease the pain of losing my child, but also that grief would become part of me. My losses would be part of my story, part of who God was leading me to become. I realized that everything had a purpose that he had not yet revealed.

Eight months after that retreat, I took a job as the liturgical coordinator at our parish and spent the next year doing the hundred and one things that needed doing to care for the sacred liturgical space used by several thousand families. One of my jobs was to handle planning parishioners' funerals. It was such a gift to me to be able to support another family walking through what I had already endured.

It took three more years before I started writing a book about my tug-of-war with God during those twenty-two years with Courtney and how I learned to trust him with every aspect of my life. Ironically, it was a book all about "being brave in the scared"—but I was terrified.

Honestly, I didn't really want to write a book. I'd never submitted anything to agents or editors, and I didn't even have a draft or an outline. But I believe that while God knew the deepest desires of my heart, he also knew my limitations. I had watched many friends—many good writers—spend years submitting their work to publishers only to be rejected. It was something I dreaded because I wasn't up to facing that possibility. So God provided another way to achieve that dream because it had always been a part of his plan.

Because I was still working on my interior life, I sometimes struggled to hear God clearly, so it was an opportunity that I almost missed. My first book, *Be Brave in the Scared*, came about because of a conversation with a friend that I thought would go nowhere. In the end, it brought about the biggest accomplishment of my life, other than being a wife and mother. All because I trusted someone with an idea, with the truth of who I was, and surrendered it to the God who loves me.

I was reluctant to share so much of my life in such a bold way, but I remember telling my editor that if we were going to dive into the truth, it would have to be the whole truth: the good, the bad, the ugly, and the even uglier. I was done hiding and overcontrolling the narrative of my life. I had come through the fire of hell, and I knew who I was, who I belonged to, and what he was asking of me. She simply said, "I know that God will work through your words and bring about a healing you don't even know you need, friend." And she was right.

I surrendered the fear of truly being known by so many one more time, secure in the knowledge that I was known by my Creator, and he was going to write this book with me. Terrified, I submitted an outline, and the project was approved. No rejection. But even after I signed the contract, I didn't feel up to the task.

As I worked on the book, however, I began to feel more at ease. By the time I was finishing up final revisions, I felt peace and contentment. While writing *Brave*, I'd been so scared, I'd surrendered completely. Within that surrender, I dumped out the most painful parts of my life's story—parts that God already knew but that I needed to write so that I could see myself as he saw me.

Letting God

How? Quite simply, I did the work of letting go and letting God. I spent time with God in adoration. I prayed. I listened. Above all, I took on the challenge that he laid at my feet. God didn't force me to write *Brave*. He gave me permission to be myself and to share from the raw and honest places. I can hear your questions now: *How do I get to know God and be known by him? What if I don't want to write a book? Or even leave the house? What opportunities do I have to surrender to God?*

It's all about relationship, friend. The peace and contentment that I finally felt came from hours spent in his

presence, reading his Word, and pouring out my prayers—
both spoken and written—over the course of more than
two decades. Strangely, much of it happened while making
mistake after mistake and poor choice after poor choice.
Yet, God remained by my side as he remains by yours,
pouring mercy after mercy, grace after grace, into a heart
that needed so much repair and restoration. By gradually
letting go of my pride and ego, I was able to set aside my
need to be perfect—or at least to look that way—and to
say yes to his plan for my life. Once I stopped fighting for
control, I was able to more easily hear him and follow his
lead.

Now don't get me wrong. Along the way, those old
wounds continued to show themselves, and at times, they
still do. The Great Deceiver wants nothing more than for
you and me to keep listening to those lies of how we are
not *fill-in-the-blank* enough. You know those lies, friend.
They're the ones that used to shout in your head, but
because you've listened to them for so long, now you are
willing to give in to them as a whisper without a fight.

Allow the voice of the Father in. Open the door to
your inner room, and let him sit with you in the broken.
Let him love you. Let him minister to your wounds and
speak truth and life over you. Step boldly into the life he
meant for you and you alone. Stop looking over the fence
at what Sally has or who Maggie is, and look into the mirror. There you will see who God is in you and understand
that you are also in him. Meet him one day at a time. Be
a woman of courage, sit in his presence, and wave your
white flag. Surrender your life to him so that he can renew,
restore, rebuild, and redeem it all.

CHAPTER 5

The Courage to Accept Love

❧

Do you believe God loves you? Your first reaction might be a resounding yes. But I'm challenging you to think deeper. Look into your heart. Do you blame God for all of your troubles? Or see him more as judge and jury and less as a merciful Father? Do you think that God loves other people more than you because they are somehow more deserving? I'll ask the question again:

Do you *really believe* that God loves *you*?

The thing about being loved by God is that the character of God never changes. His entire being is love, and he loves without boundary or condition. Humans aren't capable of unlimited generosity. So accepting God's kind of love? Well, it's a struggle. Why? Because God's love is unconditional, while the kind of love we experience here on earth comes with a list of checkboxes. Our love requires something in return, while God's is freely given without any expectations or requirements.

To allow myself to be fully and unconditionally loved by God, I had to give up all of my preconceived notions about what being loved by God even means. It means that even in my sin and depravity, God loves me with wild abandon. Great. But I still had to unpack this concept in my head, and then receive it in my heart. It sounds so simple—to understand and receive unconditional love—but it's the hardest part of this journey. That's why it took me years to understand and another decade to receive. And I'm not the most patient woman.

Ruled by Fear

When you are ruled by fear, every situation you face takes on a level of high drama that could win you an Oscar or a trip to the psych ward for the multiple personalities you may display over the course of a single day. When you constantly doubt yourself and God's plan for your life, questioning every twist and turn of the story, you end up exhausted physically and emotionally, with your dry bones rattling in the wind.

After that first Mass with Jerry, as we dated, I battled every day not to give in to the voice of the Deceiver, who would whisper lies on repeat.

You are not enough.
He will leave you for someone better.
You don't deserve him.

It sounded like the scratchy old vinyl 45s I had in high school. I didn't trust what I saw in front of me. I didn't believe that I was good enough or deserving enough to keep my handsome midshipman. I knew there were other women who were smarter and more beautiful and cultured than I was waiting in the wings. A desperation to keep Jerry interested in me surfaced. Over time, that lack of trust in myself and the woman God made me to be led me to choose lust over love. I was willing to give myself away for the *possibility* that Jerry would stay. The difference between the love I could offer and the love given by the Father was as stark as black and white. Mine required a self-addressed stamped envelope; God's required nothing in return.

A Dust Bowl Adventure

The constant buzz of desperation sounded like an old air conditioner on a hot summer day. You just got used to it. It surged to the forefront, though, in December 1986, as I was going to visit my future husband's family in Oklahoma. Jerry and I weren't yet engaged, so the stakes were high. I wanted to prove to them that I belonged—that I was worthy of their son.

I was hesitant to go because the first time I had met Jerry's parents during their visit to the Naval Academy had been less than successful. It was awkward with a capital A, and as usual, I had overcompensated by being annoyingly loud and *very* engaging. His mother had said I was "a bit much, but cute." At dinner, his father had pointed out that I had "a lot of opinions for someone so young." I didn't think that was a compliment, and neither did Jerry.

This was, however, the logical next step in our relationship. So, I swallowed my nerves, took lots of deep breaths to control my pounding heart, and came up with a plan of action to alleviate any awkwardness on this trip. I was determined to avoid embarrassing myself and overwhelm them with my awesomeness. Did I pray about that meeting? Nope. Did I ask God to bless it, to guide my words and my actions? That's a negative. Did I strive to place anyone else's needs above my own? Heck no. I was on the "I" train, and there was no one in my way.

We began the great Oklahoma adventure on the day after Christmas. Jerry and I landed in Tulsa (my first airplane ride ever!), and his parents picked us up. We spent the night at his parent's house under strict supervision, mind you. (No hanky-panky at Don and Eleanor's.) Then we were off to western Oklahoma to visit Jerry's grandmother and meet the extended family. This was not exactly my agenda, but I was swept along for the ride through the Dust Bowl.

While we drove for six hours across the wilds of the state, I got the total Lenaburg low-down. *All the deets.* Needless to say, in my enthusiasm to absorb all things Lenaburg, I was loud, talkative, and opinionated as always, about things I had no knowledge of . . . and then loud some more. It was what I did to earn the right to be loved—survivor mode in overdrive is the most unflattering part of my personality. At one point Jerry's dad, in his usual blunt way, informed me that I needed to calm down a little bit; it was going to be a long car ride out to Vici, Oklahoma. I felt like a small child being told to hush because the important people were talking, and I was not one of them. I held Jerry's hand a little tighter in the back seat, but he was oblivious. He was too involved in conversation with his sister to see the panic rising on my face. The plan I had made to overwhelm his family with awesome was slowly falling apart, and he didn't seem to care a whit about it.

By the time we pulled up to his grandmother's house late that evening, I was happy to put some space between his parents and me. I was in a whole new world, not a city light or strip mall to be found. I couldn't see much of anything but the stars. It was so quiet; all I heard was a cow mooing off in the distance. We were in the-middle-of-nowhere Oklahoma, somewhere on the Trail of Tears, and all I wanted to do was cry. These were not my people, and I had no idea how I was going to survive the next few days.

The next day, Jerry's mom and grandmother started cooking in the kitchen. I thought this would be my in. I had taken over a lot of the kitchen duties from my mom when I was in high school because I loved to cook and bake. My happy place was feeding people, and I thought it would be a chance to share that part of me with Jerry's family. I walked in and offered to help peel potatoes or shuck corn or whatever.

I was shooed out of the kitchen so fast it made my head spin.

These women had their own way of doing things, their own language between them, and I was just a complete stranger who had shown up with their baby boy and grandson. They didn't know me or my skills; this was their kitchen, and I had no place in it. I was not a member of Club Lenaburg yet.

I decided to take a walk outside with Jerry around his grandmother's farm. After all, there was a barn and maybe a little privacy away from his family. This place was so far out in the boonies that his grandmother couldn't even get a television signal (yes, this was in the days before cable). I mean, seriously, if you took the TV antenna and stood with it at just the right angle, you *might* get a picture.

I was also a little worried about something else. All morning long, his family had talked about when his great uncles were coming over to play dominoes and how "adding up spots" would be a rite of passage for me. Great, math. I couldn't wait.

Cow Pies and Dominoes

Outside I noticed a half-dozen cows standing at the fence. Okay, this was it; I was going pass from city slicker to genuine country girl and show them that I could fit in. So I asked to go and pet the cows. Jerry looked at me with genuine surprise on his face and informed me that they typically just ate them and there was no petting involved. He was working really hard at keeping a straight face, but I was determined and pushed on to the fence. When I reached out my hand to pet the cow, she just stood there and stared at me blankly. I looked at Jerry and asked why the cow was just staring at me.

He explained, in his newly rediscovered Oklahoma drawl, that the cow was waiting to be fed. He pointed to the hay bale at the end of the fence and said the cows only came to the fence when it was close to chow call. His cousin would be arriving shortly to handle that chore. Then he told me to watch my step, that there were landmines all round.

Landmines? Are we in a war zone? I thought. (Actually, I felt like I was.)

I looked down, and sure enough, there was my very first cow pie. I was fascinated—I mean, really fascinated, because it looked like a giant brown cinnamon roll. Weird, right? And before I could stop and think, I just blurted out,

"So how do they get it to look like that? Do they walk in a circle while they poop?"

I thought Jerry was going to explode.

He started laughing so hard, it looked as if he was going to roll on the ground. Actual tears were coming from his eyes, and I'm sure the confused look on my face made him laugh even harder. He informed me that in fact they just stood there and let it drop. No walking in circles was required.

We were now discussing the physics of cow poop; this was not going as I had intended. Jerry had a very mischievous look on his face that I had seen a time or three, and so I suspected trouble was coming. I threatened him that if he told anyone back at the house how country illiterate I was, there would be no making out after dinner. He just kept laughing.

All the way back I was in fear of mortal embarrassment. Seriously, how much of a city slicker could I be? This plan to be loved and accepted was going to hell in a handbasket, and fast!

And then it happened.

As soon as we came in the back door, Jerry busted out laughing again and retold the tale in his loudest voice to all his now-assembled relatives. He didn't skip a beat. He gave *all* the details and even walked in a circle while sharing his favorite line about cows pooping in circles. And, of course, the *entire* houseful of people burst out laughing at this city girl's first encounter with a cow pie. I was mortified: I mean red-faced, hands-shaking, heart-racing, going-to-kill-him-in-his-sleep mortified. Acceptance was already an uphill battle, and Jerry just kept piling it on. I couldn't believe he had told the story after I had asked him not to.

His great uncles looked at me with great amusement and then invited me to the dominoes game. I didn't know what else to do, so I took a few deep breaths on my way over, and I begged God to send a hailstorm or a field fire—anything—to get me the heck out of this. That did not go well either. You've heard of card sharks? Well, these old geezers were domino sharks, ready to take on a classic dyslexic like me. I lost every single game, and I heard about it every time I miscounted the spots.

Did I mention that I hate to lose? It makes me feel small and unworthy, and I was already in the deep pit of humiliation and embarrassment. Everyone loves a winner, right? So instead of going with the flow, I doubled down on my distaste for all things rural. I wasn't allowed in the kitchen, I wasn't good at any of the things they enjoyed, and there were cows pooping everywhere. I felt totally alone and unloved. It's funny, because now my reaction just sounds immature and whiny.

As we said goodnight a little while after the domino fiasco, Jerry told me he loved me. I simply scoffed, turned my back, went to my room, and left him standing there gawking. I was convinced that he didn't love me. You don't embarrass someone you love.

As I tried to go to sleep on the Walmart blow-up mattress jammed between the dresser and the wall of his grandmother's guest room, I thought back to the first time I was embarrassed by someone I thought cared about me.

Seven Minutes in Hell

It was my freshman year of high school and the first time a boy had invited me to a high school party. L was tall and funny, and he lived in my neighborhood. We were friends, but I really wanted to be more, even though I was fourteen and didn't really know what *more* meant. Maybe it was because he spoke kindly or that he looked like a young Denzel Washington, but when he walked me home from school or met me at the library to study, my heart beat a little faster, and I laughed a little too loudly.

At that fateful Saturday night party, we drew each other's names in a game of "Seven Minutes in Heaven." Into the closet we went. I told him no funny stuff was allowed, and he respected that—at least for the first five minutes. He sat over by the winter coats, and I was on top of the shoe rack. We talked about the science test we had coming upon Monday and the Cowboys/Redskins game the next day. Then he finally looked at me and told me we might as well get it over with. I knew he meant that we needed to kiss. That was always the finale of those darn seven minutes. In what would be the most epic kiss of my life, I leaned in and so did he.

Unfortunately, neither one of us was very skilled at this whole kissing thing, and both of us had metal braces. Orthodontically speaking, it was railroad central in that closet. As he approached me for the kiss, our lips parted, and you can just imagine what happened next. Our braces got caught. I mean they intermingled somehow, and when I pulled away 1.82 seconds later, his mouth came with me.

I began to hyperventilate. We were stuck, and neither one of us could figure out how to get unstuck. What happened during the next thirty minutes was traumatic enough to scar me for life. Kids were laughing hysterically. Praise the Lord there was no social media then, because that would have taken it to a whole other level of horrific.

My dad was called, and he showed up fifteen minutes later with a pair of needle-nose pliers and a face full of rage. He clipped us apart, then took L aside and sternly lectured him on how he expected his daughter to be treated in the future. I was mortified because it wasn't L's fault; it was the fault of those ugly braces I didn't even want.

My dad took me, my busted braces, and my too-tight Calvin Kleins home, all the while informing me that I would have to pay for whatever it cost to fix the braces. He also laid down the new rules he expected me to follow as far as attending high school parties with boys was concerned. As I walked into the house, my older brother started laughing because the news was already traveling around the school gossip channels.

L avoided me from that point on. He had been my friend, but in one seven-minute stretch, that all went away. I was a laughingstock, and for the remainder of my high school experience, I never again attended a boy-girl party or played seven minutes of anything.

A New and Improved Plan

As that memory rolled over my heart that first night in western Oklahoma, I formulated a new plan to survive the week ahead. I called it "Operation Win Them Over," and it involved me being very compliant and very quiet while doing whatever was asked of me. I felt the need to be very small because I really loved Jerry (even though he could be such a stupid boy sometimes). If his family didn't love me, then it wouldn't be possible to make this work.

The next day, I made no waves. No yelling during dominoes, no loud laughter, no pushing my way into the kitchen. Instead, I offered to do the dishes, which was greeted with thunderous gratitude. As everyone played in the dining room, I washed and dried and put away my heart with every plate.

After two days, Jerry asked if I was feeling ill because I had been so quiet. I smiled and said I was homesick; after all, it had been the first time I had traveled so far from my family alone. He told me I wasn't alone because I had him. And he really believed that. I did not. Once again, the lie of unworthiness, the lie that I was not good enough, sunk into my bones. I wanted nothing more than to leave and never come back. I had tried to be who I thought Jerry's family wanted me to be, and it was a failure. It was clear that these people weren't going to love me, and they weren't going to accept me being in Jerry's life. I was too much, too different from them. My dream of being loved unconditionally was falling away.

When we returned home, I threw myself into school and put some emotional distance between me and Jerry. I know now that I was pouting like a preschooler. But then, I thought I was entitled to feeling set aside and unloved. After dinner one night, my father asked what was bothering me. I told him that Jerry loved his family more than he loved me and that I was always going to be second. Dad laughed and told me that for the time being I should be second because I wasn't his wife. He went on to caution me that if we did marry, I should not fall into the trap of making Jerry choose between his mother and me. Dad spoke about how love required sacrifice and the ability to put the needs of another before your own. Then he asked me quite directly if I was prepared to do that for Jerry, to place his needs above mine. I was silent.

Worthy of Sacrifice

Love equals sacrifice. I had heard that for years with regard to Jesus' sacrifice on the Cross, but this was the first time I was told that I would have to sacrifice for someone I loved.

To be loved meant that someone had found me worthy of sacrifice.

To love meant that I had decided to make someone else more important than myself.

It was a watershed moment—and I had a choice to make. If I wanted to be Jerry's wife and have any shot at a peaceful existence with our extended family, I needed to understand what love was and what it wasn't. I could not enter marriage thinking that I could or should change the man I professed to love. I had to accept him and his family as they were and stop trying to mold them according to my preferences. I had to set aside my expectations and lean in to God's expectations for me—and boy, was I unprepared to hear those. My lack of maturity at the time, both emotionally and spiritually, was on full display.

It's funny. Our world throws out the word *love* like it's free and costs nothing, when in actuality love will cost you everything. Think of Jesus on the Cross. He chose us out of love, and look what it cost him—his very life.

And then there is that awesome scripture passage that so many of us women bristle at whenever we hear it read at Mass. It's Ephesians 5:21–28, and it's a doozy.

> Be subordinate to one another out of reverence for Christ. Wives should be subordinate to their husbands as to the Lord. For the husband is head of his wife just as Christ is head of the church, he himself the savior of the body. As the church is subordinate to

Christ, so wives should be subordinate to their husbands in everything. Husbands, love your wives, even as Christ loved the church and handed himself over for her to sanctify her, cleansing her by the bath of water with the word, that he might present to himself the church in splendor, without spot or wrinkle or any such thing, that she might be holy and without blemish. So [also] husbands should love their wives as their own bodies. He who loves his wife loves himself.

I know; it's a lot. I was so not in the mood to be subordinate to anyone, let alone Jerry. I had so much to learn in the love arena. Now when I read it, I see what God was saying. I was to love Jerry and be "under his mission." At the same time, Jerry was being called to love me as Christ loved the Church. How did Jesus love the Church? He gave his life on the Cross. He died for love. Jerry was being called to die for love, and apparently I was not on board with that because I had no understanding of it. Until I did. When that understanding finally made its way from my head to my heart, how I saw Jerry and his family changed as well.

People can only give you what they themselves have been given. If what they have been given is lacking, then what they give will not be complete. In order to love, I had to find the courage to receive the unconditional and sacrificial love that God—and Jerry—wanted to give me. That lesson took me twenty-two years to learn.

CHAPTER 6

the Courage to Forgive

༄

Jerry and I married in August 1988. We set off on a grand adventure, which continues to this day. He became a Naval Flight Officer in the US Navy. I gave birth to our son, Jonathan, while we were stationed in Brunswick, Maine, where Jerry deployed twice with P-3 Orion Squadron VP-11. We maintained some distance from both of our families to forge our own way on the journey of parenthood. Our daughter, Courtney, followed two and a half years later. That's when things really changed.

At five weeks old, our daughter began having grand-mal seizures. Shortly afterward, we moved to Washington, DC, for our next duty station. While we were thrilled to be with family for support, my dad was battling non-Hodgkin's lymphoma, and Jerry's godfather, Roy, was dealing with pancreatic cancer. We were under serious financial strain, and our marriage had become a dumpster fire

fueled by addictions to food and porn. Caring for Courtney was exhausting and overwhelming, a full-time job I
felt ill-qualified for. Our son was getting lost in the shuffle.
Both of our extended families had strong opinions about
what we should do and how we should do it.

For the next seven years, Courtney was in and out
of the hospital with surgeries and therapy appointments,
pneumonia and influenza, even H1N1 swine flu. She
attended a special school for severely disabled children
while I homeschooled Jonathan. We were drowning in this
new normal—as well as huge amounts of medical debt—
until we made a pilgrimage to Lourdes, France.

That trip to Lourdes changed the course of our family's life, and who we are today is a direct result of Our
Lady's mercy. She surrounded us with love and breathed
courage into our hearts. But even with changed hearts, our
problems didn't go away. I was still seeking that love that
seemed so unreachable. After grasping for so many things
to fill that hole for so long, I gave in, gave up, and turned in
on myself. Those were dark years filled with pain and hurt
buried so deep that I'm still dealing with the scar tissue.

Hurtful Words

My relationship with Jerry's parents, Don and Eleanor,
didn't start off great (remember how opinionated I was
for someone so young?), and it never really improved. I
spent a dozen years dancing around my in-laws, trying
not to offend them, and mostly failing. And that dance
was mutual. I didn't trust them, and they didn't trust me.
We were like two lions circling each other, roaring loudly

from time to time, to make sure the other cat paid attention. Things fell apart the night of Jonathan's Confirmation.

Our eighth-grade son was excited to receive his Confirmation. Courtney was eleven, and her seizures made it impossible for her to remain quiet during Mass. Eleanor and Don had come into town for the event, and it had been a stressful visit. They criticized every parenting choice we made and proffered their unsolicited opinions loudly and often—until the walls crumbled.

After reminding me that Courtney would never be able to play with her cousins or get married or have a baby, Eleanor admitted that she and Don were upset that Courtney would never have a normal life. They went on to say that they couldn't figure out what sin they had committed to bring Courtney's illness upon the family. I am not kidding. I may have sharpened my knives—and then pulled out the rat poison. I'm not actually sure, because I think I blacked out from rage. Finally, when I was able to speak again, I asked Eleanor if she thought Courtney was a mistake. I dared my mother-in-law to say the word. Instead of backing down, she kept at it. She was sure that Courtney's imperfections were due to some sin or mistake or grave misdeed committed somewhere along the family line.

Even though Jerry had stepped in between us—mostly to prevent me from going to prison for assault or worse—I had enough of my wits left to respond with a scripture passage. Specifically, John 9:1–3: "As he passed by he saw a man blind from birth. His disciples asked him, 'Rabbi, who sinned, this man or his parents, that he was born blind?' Jesus answered, 'Neither he nor his parents sinned; it is so that the works of God might be made visible through him.'"

I desperately needed Eleanor to understand that the glory of God could be revealed through Courtney. But then I launched my own attack and accused Eleanor of never welcoming me into the family. I wanted her to admit that, as far as she was concerned, I'd never been enough for her son—that they didn't love me. When I was done, I'd not only dumped all of my own insecurities and pain on her, I had also made sure that my in-laws knew that, while they could come at me, Courtney was off-limits.

Standing Together

Jerry and I were astounded that his parents had no clue about how God saw our family. We weren't perfect, but we were his. We belonged to him and he to us. Courtney and Jonathan were God's gifts for us to receive and love. My in-laws could not see or know Courtney as we did, and that is why they couldn't love her as we did. As a lifelong Catholic, I was shocked to discover that they had no understanding of redemptive suffering. But since God makes all things good, he did give me one gift that night.

He gave me Jerry.

For the first time in our marriage, Jerry stood up for me. He made sure that they realized Courtney was a gift, not a curse. He made sure they realized that God gave Courtney to us out of love and not as a punishment.

The words exchanged that night forever changed the course of my relationship with my in-laws. It was one of the most painful moments in my life. Since I didn't accept responsibility for any of it, I absolved myself. But an encounter like that only happens after a long history of misunderstandings and harsh judgments—on both sides. Because the wounded always wound others.

My in-laws left the next day, and I had little to no contact with them for two years. At the request of his sister, Jalanna, Jerry spoke to them periodically. Today I am grateful for Jalanna's wise council and steadfast friendship. She loved us all, and it broke her heart to see family division. Despite having her own issues with her parents, Jalanna could see what I could not: Eleanor's need to be known and loved in return.

After those two years, we settled into a détente where calls and cards were once more exchanged. I kept things pleasant and light, but I never asked about anything important. I couldn't risk the hurt and pain. Meanwhile, Jerry and I recommitted ourselves to God and were determined to survive whatever storms life pitched our way. God healed, redeemed, and restored our marriage. We still stumbled and made mistakes, but we remained committed to each other. Jerry knew my deepest secrets and my darkest sins. Yet he still remained, by my side, loving me through it all. I returned that love and devotion in equal measure.

Jerry had become my safe haven and I his strong tower. For the first time in our marriage, we had each other's backs. We rooted for each other, wanting the other to become the best version of themselves. In him I saw strength and honor, wisdom and deep faith. He'd finally become our family's spiritual leader, and I had Courtney to thank for it.

Yet while we fought for our hard-won happy marriage, our daughter never had to do anything to earn our love. With her profound disabilities she—literally—couldn't do anything except love, and she loved freely and fully without reservation. Jerry and I had first thought of love as something to be earned or won. When I fully understood how Courtney loved, I realized that God loved me the same way.

God knew us before time began and set his affections for us. He made us out of love and for love. We just have to believe it to receive it.

No Room for Bitterness

In the summer of 2014, our world took yet another turn. Courtney's health declined, and the doctors informed us that her remaining time was short. Jerry and I knew that we had to reconcile with his family. Goodbyes needed to be said and forgiveness offered. And I had to figure out a way to let this happen without rancor or bitterness.

Jerry's parents and sister arrived on a crisp October morning. From the beginning, things felt different. They walked with a peace and reverence that I'd never seen before. They weren't here for me, and I prayed that the Lord would hold my tongue so I would not screw up whatever grace he wanted to give us with this visit.

That evening my in-laws took Courtney in their arms and sat with her. They told her how proud they were of her and how hard she had fought. Honestly, if I hadn't seen it myself, I wouldn't have believed it. They asked her forgiveness for anything they might have said or done to hurt her feelings and told her that, because of her, they'd learned how to love in a deeper way. That night Eleanor sang Courtney to sleep, rocking her back and forth while softly singing, "You Are My Sunshine," the song Eleanor sang over Courtney at her birth.

After I tucked Courtney into bed, my mother-in-law took my hand and quietly cried by Courtney's bedside. My father-in-law appeared and put his arm around me. Shocked, I took a deep breath and asked God into this moment. That's when Eleanor admitted that Courtney had changed their hearts and brought them closer to God. Courtney's courage and strength in this earthly fight had inspired them—yet they were still brokenhearted about the time they had wasted. That's when Eleanor asked for my forgiveness.

My heart broke. And in the breaking, I released all of the resentment and unforgiveness that had bound me. But when Eleanor and Don told me that they loved me, I couldn't speak. Finally, the Holy Spirit showed up and gave me the courage to apologize for my own actions and immaturity. When I told them I loved them, I meant it.

Jerry's parents loved me, and they loved my daughter. In a single breath, the greatest desire of my heart had been fulfilled. And it had taken only twenty-two years. These two people whose love and respect I had desired for so long stood with me in the darkest moments of my motherhood with no judgment, no fraternal correction, just acceptance. Death changes people. It makes us realize that we are not long for this world. We all acknowledged how much time we had wasted judging or trying to change one another when we could have been working together as a team. What did it cost to let go of decades of resentment and hurt? Only pride.

Making Up for Lost Time

Over the next two years, we grew closer until the death of my father-in-law on December 27, 2016. Yes, you read that correctly; it was the same date as our Courtney, only two years later. But within those two dates, God wrote a story of redemption and remembrance.

In November 2019, we made our way to Oklahoma for Thanksgiving with all of the Lenaburgs. Jerry planned our trip like a covert operation. It was a surprise for Eleanor, who by then was in assisted living. When she saw all of us in her room, she cried and hugged everyone—even me. But the best part of that whole weekend was that I finally got to be in charge of the Lenaburg kitchen. Yup. Thirty-one years later I was in the kitchen cooking while Eleanor soaked in the love of her children and grandchildren.

It was a week of *so* much joy and laughter, one I will treasure until my last breath. As I watched my son and husband dote on Eleanor, I whispered words of thanksgiving to my daughter. We were all there because Courtney had shown us the way. God's constancy and faithfulness brought us home, even if it took decades to get there.

My sincerest hope for you, friend, is that you will not have to wait as long as I did. Be bold, my friend, and let go of the resentments that keep you from unconditional love.

CHAPTER 7

The Courage to Belong

~∾

At the beginning of this book, I shared with you the most-asked question I hear when I'm on the road speaking: "What does God want of me?" My answer is still the same: *holiness.*

But Mary, I still don't get it? How do I achieve holiness?

It's a lifelong journey with so many pit stops along the way. Holiness is all about discovering how to see God, learning how to know him, and figuring out how to love him. It's all about being more like him, from the inside out.

Once you realize that God sees you, knows you, and loves you first, you'll understand what he wants of you. It'll come to you in one of the quiet conversations you'll have together—the kind of chat one has with a dear friend like Jesus. Or it'll come to you as a flash of insight into your mind—the kind of spontaneous idea the Holy Spirit is famous for. Or it'll come to you in a chance meeting with others—the kind of coincidence God loves to facilitate.

Or maybe you'll be sitting in prayer or adoration or just appreciating the beauty of a flower, when you're suddenly filled with peace because you just know that you belong.

Sounds simple, right?

Except we all know it's not. Because of our brokenness and the baggage we carry from old wounds and past mistakes, we don't remember how to listen. We miss those small opportunities to learn what God wants for us. We forget to whom we belong.

Welcomed as You Are

We all desire to belong to a family, a church, a team. We ache to belong to others who accept us as we are—those unique and prized individuals who want you to be part of their lives without requiring you to change. Yet we waste time trying to fit in with all the wrong people and for all the wrong reasons. I spent most of my life turning myself into a human pretzel so I would be accepted by others. We all do this. We have a deep, emotional instinct to belong— to peer groups, our work environment, an athletic team, even a church group.

What's even harder is finding a place you belong and then discovering that you have to leave.

When Jerry resigned from the Navy, we landed in northern Virginia. We had left behind our B Street crew, who had been such a balm to our hearts. Some of those couples remain in our lives today. They were our first wall of defense when we were both deep in addiction and fighting internal battles they had no idea about. They just loved us where we were. God knew we needed a lifeboat, and these friends provided a safe landing in the midst of great storms.

The move was hard on all of us because we didn't know what the future held. At the time, Jerry and I were still struggling in our marriage, and Jonathan and Courtney had their own challenges. Courtney was six and Jonathan almost nine when we rented a small townhouse. I was worried that we would not find a new church or friends and terrified that we wouldn't belong.

Dress for Distress

Soon after the move was the first time I tried to find an outfit for a corporate event. My husband had just gotten a promotion, and there was a big family picnic being put on by the company at a local state park.

Panic ensues: I have nothing to wear. Everything in my closet says I'm going to church or I'm going to work out or I'm cleaning the bathroom. I struggle to find the perfect "I belong here" outfit without breaking my very tight budget.

I scour my stack of catalogs trying to avoid that darn dressing room one more time, but alas, it's not to be. I hit the mall, and the hunt begins. I find a fabulous pair of cropped gingham trousers in the lightest shade of petal pink that are preppy and cute. Better still, I can button them without passing out. I let the sales lady talk me into a linen blouse that I know will be lovely, but I worry about the wrinkles. Still, I buy it because she has all the confidence, and I have none.

Next up come the shoes. I am such an accessories junkie! I love shoes and jewelry and scarves as well as a fabulous handbag. I think I could wear head-to-toe black everyday if it meant I could spice it up with bright, fabulous accessories. But I digress. Shoes do that to me. They are very distracting.

I need something sensible and comfortable, but also something that will make a statement that says, "I belong here." That's a lot of pressure for a shoe, but I am determined. I try on everything that the four major department stores have in stock and try to decide between three styles that have caught my eye.

There is a cute pair of ballet flats in a stunning shade of melon. They fit and are quite sensible but make my ankles look thick. They're screaming, "I am a sensible seventy-five-year-old grandma who has bunions and can't wear a heel anymore!" Too soon for those. I need to be hip and youthful like everyone I am sure to meet at this picnic. I was neither, but I knew I could be if only I wore the right pair of shoes.

Next I step into a truly righteous sandal with a square one-inch heel and a strap around the ankle with silver buckle to the side. They are the shade of a pink peony at full bloom in spring. I actually sigh when I think of them with my new trousers. As much as I love them, all I can imagine is the pedicure that would be required, and there is no time or money for that, so I move on.

I stumble upon a classic espadrille in the color of eggshell. I feel as if I'm walking on pillows and nothing is rubbing the wrong way. The color is a risky choice given that the picnic is at a state park, but Jerry had said there was a pavilion, so I decide in that moment that these beauties are mine. At 40 percent off, they do indeed belong on my feet.

I remember what it felt like to belong when we lived in Norfolk, and I want that feeling back pronto. This is our chance. The boys have new golf shirts and pressed khaki shorts. Courtney has a new sundress and sweater that compliments her hat and wheelchair color, because clashing with your wheelchair is just not done. I am pressed and prettied and ready to dazzle.

Outsiders

Within the first ten minutes of arriving to this corporate event, I knew I had made a horrific mistake. I did not belong there. First, there were *no* other children there even though it was a family picnic, and second, there were only a few wives. Everyone was playing volleyball and badminton like we do at our family picnics. But there were kegs of beer and three different BBQ pits going with various meats, and everyone from the president of the company to those in the secretarial pool were dressed in cutoff jeans and sneakers. There was no pavilion in what was basically a big open field. We stuck out like a sore thumb. I had made a monumental mistake, and all I wanted to do was run.

Regrettably, it would look even worse if we did, so Jerry said we had to stay for at least an hour. It was already a disaster, though, and I didn't want to push it. I gathered the children under a shade tree and quietly asked Jerry to bring us a plate so I could at least give the kids some lunch before we ran away. He did, and then went off to "work the room."

Misery never had better company. It was horrid, and I thought nothing could be worse—until Jerry brought

the president of the company over to meet the family. As
I stood up, I fumbled Courtney's hot dog, which promptly
plopped onto my new, pristine, eggshell espadrilles. As I
watched the ketchup and mustard mingle with my humiliation, I quickly snapped my head back up in the most fake
smile ever and chatted with the gentleman, totally ignoring
the slimy feeling on my foot. Once his boss went back to
the festivities, I told Jerry we were out of there. We did not
belong here.

I know what you're thinking, *Why so dramatic, Mary?*
It felt like every other time our family tried to fit in. Everyone always stared. If Courtney made a sound, we got the
look. We were either underdressed or overdressed. And I
was hyperaware of all these things because we *were* different without ever having to *do anything to be* different. It
was my childhood all over again.

Just as You Are

But that's the difference between fitting in and belonging,
isn't it? Fitting in means you change yourself for someone
else, and belonging is when you are welcomed just as you
are. I desperately wanted to belong, but I couldn't even get
it right for a flippin' picnic. How was I ever going to get
it right for the really important stuff? I wanted my family to belong just as we were, so I hoped that God would
fix it—more like "fix us"—because I was ready to give up
again. What I really needed was the courage *not* to fit in,
the guts to stand out, and the audacity to be bold—even
in the broken.

CHAPTER 8

The Courage to Be Vulnerable

❧

Starting over again is never easy. Actually, let's just call a spade a spade. Starting over again sucks noodles, and it was getting old. Every day felt like the first day of classes in a brand-new school. It reminded me of my junior high years, which had been filled with so much stress, sweat socks, and strife.

I grew tired of putting on mask after mask to fit someone else's ideal, to be who someone else thought I should be. I wanted to wear my flannel shirt and leggings and embrace my Mrs. Claus physique. The fact is that I never felt safe enough to do that outside of my own home. I wanted my kids to be included and not feel like outsiders wherever they went. But I was tired of having to try so hard. I wanted to be accepted without having to change one hair on my head. I wanted to belong.

When we first arrived in northern Virginia, I was not in a good headspace. I was worried and defensive about how our family would be perceived, and that pushed me to that familiar place of grasping and overreaching in order to be deemed worthy of belonging.

It started when we found a new parish to attend. There was a group of homeschooling families who had welcomed us warmly. It was a relief for a while, until things started to get sticky. Always too loud and too proud, I clashed with some of the moms and so did my son. We were already the odd family out because of our Courtney, but this was different. It felt like I was the square peg constantly trying to fit into the round hole.

Courtney was attending a special-needs school to ensure that she would receive her physical and occupational therapy as well as other services she qualified for because of her disabilities. We had decided to homeschool Jonathan in the second grade for several reasons, but the primary one was behavioral. He just did better in a quieter environment where he could learn at his own speed and not be forced to conform to a schedule with less challenging academics and lots of "sitting still" time. Like his father, Jonathan was highly intelligent, but that didn't help the social awkwardness of my then ten-year-old.

Serving the Altar

One thing that most of the homeschooled Catholic boys in our area shared was serving at Mass. My brothers had all been altar servers. In my book, it was a sacred duty and a way to serve your parish. So when Jonathan came of age, I asked if he wanted to serve. He gave a resounding yes, and off to training he went.

Jonathan was not known for his ability to sit still. In that department, he was truly my doppelganger. He struggled a bit during the training, and the young priest who was training him was not known for his patience. But Jonathan hung in there and was finally allowed to serve his first daily Mass.

Watching him serve was torture for me. Everyone could see every move he made, correct or not, and I begged God the entire time to help him not to mess up. We got through an entire week of daily Masses and finally arrived at his first Sunday Mass. He was feeling confident, and I had already started interceding for him three days prior. Our whole family would be on display, bless it.

Warning: If you are a mom of a young person who is training to serve as an altar server, go ahead and skip this part. Everything went beautifully. There, you don't need to stress.

For the rest of you, Jonathan was doing great during the entrance hymn and the opening of the Mass. Then it came time for the Proclamation of the Word, and everyone sat down while the deacon read the Gospel. Then came the homily. It was a warm day, and the air conditioning was not keeping up with the humidity of the Virginia summer. Father was on fire with his homily, but he was having trouble landing the plane and went on for more than twenty minutes. As he was winding up, I looked over and watched in horror as Jonathan was slumped over in his chair, sound asleep and snoring. Loudly.

The altar servers next to him were all smiles trying not to laugh. Then the one next to Jonathan nudged him, and my deepest fears came to life before my eyes. Jonathan fell over into the potted plant that was next to him,

making the most incredible racket imaginable. There were
gasps and whispers, but the best part was when Jonathan
said in a very loud voice, "Damn. My mom's going to kill
me." He righted the plant with dirt all over the carpet and
promptly sat down. I can still physically feel the ripple that
made its way through the congregation. I bowed my head
in mortification and remembered the first time I had felt
this way at Mass.

Fourth-Grade Fiasco

I was in the fourth grade, and Mrs. LaFlame had asked me
to be the reader for our class Mass. I was honored, excited,
and terribly nervous because I wasn't the best reader. Even
worse, the reading was from Ecclesiastes, and I couldn't
spell it, let alone pronounce it correctly. I practiced for
days, reading and rereading in my room. When the day
arrived, my knees were visibly knocking together under
my box-pleat jumper uniform.

I got to the ambo and stepped up onto the milk crate,
so I was tall enough to reach the mic. I was slow, method-
ical, and measured in my speech. I made it through the
reading with only one minor mistake and was so relieved
that I forgot I was on the milk crate. When I moved, I fell
and cracked my head on the marble altar floor. The sound
of every mother's gasp at that moment came flooding back
to me as Jonathan's mistake made its way through the congregation.

Just like my son, I got up holding my head and made
my way back to my seat, trying not to cry. So many eyes
were on me. Besides the pounding rhythm of my heartbeat
that brought more discomfort with it, all I heard was one

of the little old ladies siting in the next row whisper about how clumsy I was and how I shouldn't be a reader if I was just going to embarrass myself.

Humiliated

My classmates never forgot that blunder. It was that *epic*. But my takeaway from that day was that I did not belong up there. I was not up to the task.

I felt my own heartbeat as Jonathan squirmed—he was completely unaware that the *entire world* was looking at him and snickering—and I was right back in the fourth grade. My head was pounding again as it had then.

In what was a visible miracle, Father kept right on going with the Mass, and the other servers went right along with him. But the worst part came after Mass, when the young priest who had trained him and had been watching the entire debacle informed Jonathan that he was done being an altar boy—and he did so in front of all the other servers in a rather loud voice.

I did not take this kindly and marched right into that sacristy, gave that young priest a piece of my mind, took my crying son by the hand, and marched out of there. It was hard and awkward and so unnecessary. All that was required was some empathy, compassion, and further training. But that was not to be. Instead there were hurt feelings, further isolation, and absolutely no belonging.

We struggled to find our balance for some time after that little disaster.

Again, I know these things happen to everyone, but when you're trying to find where you belong, when you are searching for a safe place to land, any little shake-up really throws a wrench into things and creates lasting pockets of doubt and fear. At this point I was swimming in it all once again.

A Welcoming Spirit

I had to learn to let go of the expectations I had of finding some mythical house of belonging and try to make my own home where people felt welcome. I couldn't control other people or their opinions of me or my family. I could just keep showing up, with my precocious ten-year-old son, my blinged-up, wheelchair-bound daughter, and a husband who wanted nothing more than to be home reading about some great battle. I felt like a salmon swimming upstream, and once I made it there was a great-big grizzly waiting for his little lunchtime snack. I just had to keep swimming.

Some relief came in the form of our little Family Group. These were other families at our parish who taught their kids religious ed at home. We gathered every Sunday after the 9 a.m. Mass at one family's home, rotating each week. We split the children up by age, and a set of parents would teach each group. Over time these families became an extension of our own. They did not seem bothered by Courtney's seizures or Jonathan's occasional outbursts or his abundant, encyclopedic knowledge of trains and dinosaurs.

These beautiful humans began to walk with us not only with prayer but with practical help as well. We looked forward to being with them every Sunday. It wasn't perfect, but it was a bit of a respite from the ever-changing landscape of our life. We felt as if maybe we had found where we belonged.

We found a note on our wheelchair van one morning after Mass. It was from Christine and Marques, the newest members of our Family Group. They invited us over for brunch—and there was maple bacon. That was all my introverted husband needed to hear. There was bacon, so we were going. From the moment Marques met us at their front door that day and then helped Jerry lift Courtney's wheelchair into the house without even blinking an eye, we have been welcome in their home.

The Gift of Vulnerability

Christine's openness to sharing their family's journey through hardships and serious difficulties allowed Jerry and me to trust them with our own story. We were open in a way that we had never been before—not with anyone. This was a soul-to-soul friendship. It went deep into the hidden woundedness of our marriage and our individual journeys of brokenness and sin.

It didn't take long for them to become our mentors and constant cheerleaders. They prayed for us, with us, and over us, and we did the same for them. There were nights when I wept on their couch trying to figure out if my marriage could be saved. There were quiet conversations between Marques and Jerry over habitual sin and chastity within marriage. There were days when Courtney would have seizures, and Marques, who had been miraculously cured of them himself in high school, would pray over her, bringing her peace. They accepted our unique family completely, with arms and hearts open wide.

We kept nothing from them: no sin, no struggle, no joy, no heartache. Never was this more valuable than when Jerry and I went through marriage counseling and therapy as the addictions that were strangling our marriage bubbled to the surface. It takes a true friend to come alongside you in your deepest vulnerability and pain. Christine and Marques dug in with us and were always ready to listen and help work through the hard things with us. We were able to be fully present to one another without embarrassment or judgment. They met us with empathy and compassion, and we did the same in return.

I'm not saying our friendship has been perfect, though. We've had times of strife and disagreements too. There have been short periods of pulling back, when old wounds or feelings of jealousy surged to the surface or when one of us really needed fraternal correction—usually me, if I am being honest. But whenever we have had disagreements, in time and through prayer, we have been able to come to the table and talk them through. Forgiveness has been both given and received. I remember one very difficult conversation between Christine and myself. We had allowed distance and time to enter in after a disagreement. Instead of just owning up to what I had said or she had done, the sun had set on our anger and frustration, which made the forgiving part a smidge more challenging. But honesty had always been the linchpin to our friendship, and once I spilled my guts and she spilled hers, we walked away as stronger friends because we knew each other's hearts so well. This is the gift of belonging in a friendship that welcomes vulnerability.

Belonging to God

God wants the same relationship with us, my friend. He desires nothing more than for you and me to share every-thing with him. Vulnerability is how we build trust. We walk together holding one another up in the hardships.

I had to find the courage to share every part of my heart with God. I had to learn to trust him with my great-est desires, despite my greatest fears. I had to learn that, even in my brokenness, he had created me to be bold.

The amazing thing is that God already knows it all. He is just waiting quietly for you to know that he knows, so that he can restore you in love and heal all the pain and hurt. He takes all the brokenness and humiliation, all the embarrassing habits and awkward behaviors, and wraps them in the complete perfection of his unconditional love. And that's when God makes his purpose clear.

loved with a Purpose

What I have realized over the course of my life is that my mission has always been the same: to love. It's not easy when you take a mirror to your soul and figure out that it's pretty much a dumpster fire that's capable of burning down the whole block. But God in his mercy and wisdom kept sending me help, kept meeting me in the midst of that internal battle, and kept providing me with unconditional love and mercy. Eventually, I began to surrender each and every vice and allowed him to heal and restore me to full health. That's what God's love can do once you find the courage to accept it.

God has remained faithful and true. His character never changes, but I have most certainly changed. I finally see it. I have been on mission this whole time, and God has used every experience, both good and bad, to prepare me for yet another new season in my life. When I was home with my Courtney, caring for her every need, living a very ordinary life, God was preparing me even then to step out and love in a bigger and bolder way—even when I'm broken.

God has always had a purpose for my life. My journey to holiness is to continue to surrender daily to what he asks me to do and to stay as close to him as I can. He calls each one of us to strive for holiness and not give in to helplessness. Nothing is wasted with God. Not. One. Thing. The life I have today is the result of walking through the fire of pride and selfishness, of learning to abide rather than grasp, and of understanding that my mission needs to be aligned with the mission that God has for me.

A Work in Progress

My daily prayer is "God, I want what you want"—at least that's what I shoot for. Most days I'm not quite there, and it sounds more like "God, help me to want what you want." The point is that I'm a work in progress, and I still make mistakes. I am and will always be a sinner. But God still pursues me and asks me to draw one step closer every day.

God continues to surprise me, and he continues to send people to help. Sharon W. has been my critique partner for fourteen years now. You are holding my *second* book in your hands because she has tirelessly encouraged me (and put up with my horrid grammar and unmatched love of dropping commas where they are not needed). That woman deserves a medal for what I have made her read over the years. But she makes me feel as if I could actually win a Pulitzer Prize. That's what God does when you are obedient to whatever he is asking of you. He sends you Sharon W. to make all the words better.

I am still stunned by the faithfulness of God. Now I get to travel and speak encouragement to men and women all over the world. It's a joy to share my journey to understanding whose I am and what I was created to do.

Belonging is a result of being seen, known, and loved by God. We belong simply because we are his children. Nothing is required of us, except to receive God's unconditional love. I just wish I had come to that knowledge a little sooner in my life; it would have saved me a lot of hardship and pain.

What about you, dear friend? Where are you today? Do you think you're too broken to be loved? Are you changing who you are to fit in? Do you struggle with knowing where you belong? Let me help you. You belong here, friend. You matter. Where we see weakness and failure, God sees strength and purpose. When we ruminate on the past, God plans a hopeful future.

You were made for greatness, and that greatness looks different for each and every one of us. That's the beauty of living a unique and unrepeatable life. No one's journey is the same. We may share similar experiences, but how God speaks to us through them and how he makes use of them will be as individual as we are.

It has been six years since our daughter's death, and I am in awe of how God has worked through every fear and each moment of humiliation. He has created a new heart in me, one that gratefully accepts who I am and where he is leading me. He has provided new guides and mentors along the way.

Not Our Ways

Some call me the "Catholic Mom of Instagram." It's a title I respect and cherish. So many young people have entered my circle of crazy and allowed me to pray for and encourage them. It's an honor and a privilege to be called anyone's mother, and I do not take that lightly. I know that I will be responsible for whatever advice I have given, and I continue to hold all who come my way close to my heart. They belong here, and I pray they each know it.

God's ways are not our ways, friend. His plans are so much bigger and better than we can ever imagine. When we yield to that plan, friend—truly yield—what comes is so much more than we thought possible.

I meditate often on Isaiah 55:8–9: "For my thoughts are not your thoughts, nor are your ways my ways—oracle of the LORD. For as the heavens are higher than the earth, so are my ways higher than your ways, my thoughts higher than your thoughts."

My ways were not God's ways for far too long. I have run in every direction possible away from him. And yet, when I was finally brave enough to stop running and turn around, when I gathered all my courage in one place, there he was waiting for me. He's waiting for you too—with arms open wide and a smile on his face.

God calls me by name and beckons me to himself. He's calling you as well.

God has shown me that his light shines brightest through the most broken parts of my life. He will shine in your brokenness too. Let him, friend.

My mission field has changed, but my mission has not. God has been very clear about what he is asking of me and has given me every tool needed to accomplish his work. But more than any work, God wants my heart. His unconditional love has strengthened my will and given me courage to speak from deep wounds that have been healed, but not forgotten.

Who I Am

I am his daughter worthy of love and respect. I am strong and bold, loud and brash, I call a spade a spade, I defend the defenseless with passion and purpose, and I love to bake and cook for my people. My happy place is at a crowded table laden with love, laughing, and belonging. I procrastinate like nobody's business, but I do get the job done (eventually). It's just kind of a tornado experience for those around me. I constantly overthink things and still look for approval from those who carry less weight than my God. But I am learning to lean in to the Cross of the One who died for all of it. My body bears a story of love for my children as well as cupcakes and pasta. I am quick-tempered but just as quick to forgive. Holding on to unforgiveness only rots the vessel in which it's contained; I ain't got time for that.

My door is always open, and you will always find a seat at my table. I speak truth into doubt, compassion into pain, and I fight fear on a daily basis. I refuse to give the deceiver any space in my head or my heart. Some days I win that battle, and some days I lose it, but God sees, knows, and loves me every day. Knowing that truth changes everything.

Hi. My name is Mary Elizabeth Lenaburg. I'm a wife and a mother. I'm an encourager and a consoler. I'm a writer and a storyteller. I speak wisdom and mercy over those who come to me seeking shelter from the storms of life. I am a daughter of the Most High King sent on mission to share the Good News and to love, inspire, and embolden all whom he places in my path. I am bold in my broken. And you can be too.

Acknowledgments

First and foremost, thank you, Jesus, for giving me yet another opportunity to share how you have transformed me from the inside out. I pray this book finds its way into the hands of all those who need to know of your love for them.

To everyone at St. Mary of Sorrows Youth Ministry: Fr. Barkett, Mark, Alice, Kathryn, Sienna, Dawn, Frances, Nick, Davide, Cathy, Dave, and all our kids past and present. Thank you for keeping me grounded and helping me see what's truly important—sharing the love of Christ with the next generations of saints.

To Jaymie Stuart Wolfe and the team at Ave Maria Press. Thanks for cheering me on to the finish line and making me look good. Jaymie, you are an editing queen, and I wouldn't be here without you. Thank you for being on my team.

Leah Darrow, thank you for your words and for your support of this project. I have learned much from you—most importantly to have confidence in who God made me to be and to never leave the house without a great pair of statement earrings. They make every situation survivable.

Thanks, Mom and Dad, for never giving up on me and loving me through all the rebellion and the heartache. Thank you for encouraging me to just be me. Always. I hope I made you proud.

To my siblings, Chris, Joe, Tim, Rich, Dave, Andy, and Marianne. You never let me settle, you challenged me to stay in the game, and you keep me humble. Thank you for always reminding me that family has always got my back.

Sharon Wray, you have encouraged me to keep writing for more than a decade now. Thank you for not letting me quit on myself or my dream. Maybe one day I'll actually figure out what a dangling participle is.

Kathryn Whitaker, you have walked by my side for six years now. I am so grateful to God for our friendship. You encourage me to embrace my unique voice, drive in my own lane, and not worry about anyone else. Maverick, you're not so bad either. Dr. Pepper and Torchy's for life!

Deacon and Christine, Nick and Frankie, Hannah, Tori, and Noah, thank you for always keeping the door open and a seat at the table for me. Thank you for walking with us through the good, the bad, and the crazy in between. Here's to Mexican Train and Memorial Day movie marathons. Love y'all to the moon and back.

My dear Courtney and Jonathan, to be your mother is pure gift. Courtney, thank you for your constant intercession from heaven. This book would not exist without it. J-man, I cannot wait to see where God leads you, son. You are such an amazing man of deep faith and honor. The future is waiting for you to take hold of it. Be bold. Be you. God's got the rest.

Jerry, my beloved, my heart. Once again you cheered me on to the finish line, through all the doubt and confusion. You never once gave up on me or our life together, no matter how dark it got. Thank you for always fighting for me. I love you now and always.

Finally to you, my dear readers. Thank you for allowing me to be a small part of your journey this side of heaven. God is good, *all* the time.

Reflection Questions

As you read through this book on your own, with a friend, or in a small group, reflect on these questions for each chapter. Space has been left so that you can note your responses for your personal reflection.

Introduction: Longing for Love

1. What is your equivalent of the Little Black Dress?

2. What are the negative whispers you hear in your head?

3. What does "the journey to holiness" mean to you?

Chapter 1: Measuring Up and Fitting In

1. In what area of your life do you compare yourself to others? How do you think God sees that area of your life?

2. What wounds from your childhood still hurt? What can you do to become open to God's healing grace for those wounds?

3. Which virtue do you most need to practice in order to assist you in discovering the truth about yourself?

4. What is the affirmation you most need to hear today? (Examples: I am capable. I am smart enough to do what I need to do and to be who I'm meant to be. "I have the strength for everything through him who empowers me" [Phil 4:13].)

Chapter 2: Love Is the Linchpin

1. Identify one of the biggest disappointments in your life. What role did your expectations play in that let down?

2. Looking back on those expectations today, were they reasonable, achievable, sustainable, or not? Where did your expectations come from?

3. Have your expectations changed? Why or why not?

4. Are you able to let go of current and past expectations and lean in to God's plan with hope?

Chapter 3: The Courage to Be Real

1. What gifts or talents do you see in yourself? Are there gifts you see in others that you desire? Have you ever been envious of someone?

2. How do you reconcile what you have with what you desire? How do you think God reconciles your gifts and limitations with your desires?

3. How do you present yourself to others? What are the things about yourself you try to hide or cover up? Why?

4. Is there someone in your life who inspires and encourages you to be your real, authentic self? Make a list of the things that person does to speak truth to you and empower you to embrace it.

Chapter 4: The Courage to Surrender

1. Have you fully accepted who God made you to be? Why or why not?

2. Have you fully embraced the life he has given you as it is? What holds you back?

3. What gets in the way of finding peace and contentment with your life as it is?

4. Find a scripture that addresses that obstacle or challenge. Ask God to speak to you through those words for the next week. Be still and listen. Write down what comes to mind in prayer.

Chapter 5: The Courage to Accept Love

1. Do you really believe that God loves you? Why or why not?

2. Do you believe that you are worthy of God's love? Why or why not?

3. Describe a moment in your life in which you knew beyond doubt that you were deeply loved.

4. How have you been able to draw from that well in order to pour God's love into where you are today?

Chapter 6: The Courage to Forgive

1. Is there someone you need to forgive? What keeps you from doing that?

2. Is there someone you need to ask for forgiveness? What keeps you from doing that?

3. What does forgiveness look like for you?

4. Have you experienced the power of forgiveness in your
    own life? How do you translate that power into your
    current relationships?

Chapter 7: The Courage to Belong

1. What do you believe God is asking of you today? Do you think it's possible?

2. What do you think is the difference between "fitting in" and "belonging"?

3. Do you often feel judged or criticized for being your authentic self? Do you find it easy or difficult to accept others without judgement or criticism?

4. How do you help others find their place and belong?

Chapter 8: The Courage to Be Vulnerable

1. What makes you feel vulnerable?

2. How large does a fear of rejection loom in your life? In what ways does that change your behavior?

3. How do you handle rejection, isolation, or embarrassment? Identify what has helped you to find a comfortable place again after a negative experience.

4. How do you cultivate a spirit of hospitality in your own
   life and relationships?

Conclusion: Loved with a Purpose

1. What mission field do you feel called to by God?

2. What does it look like for you to trust God in your daily mission?

3. Are you open to God using not only your gifts but also your woundedness, limitations, and failures for your good and his glory?

**READ ON FOR A PREVIEW OF
MARY LENABURG'S BOOK**

BE BRAVE
IN THE SCARED

CHAPTER ONE

OUT OF CONTROL

Control is power. When we have a plan, we can tell ourselves that we are in charge of our lives. It's easy to be brave. We feel confident when we know what to expect. After all, things are locked down. Expectations are met. Everything is bright and shiny. But control is a funny thing. One minute unicorns roam the world, flowers fall from the sky, and cupcakes don't have calories. The next minute a thundering herd of rhinos trample all our delusions, and we are left vulnerable and afraid.

To be in control means believing you're directing your path and making the right choices. That's why many of us are, well, controlling. The best part of being a control freak? Everyone around you respects you and your decisions. They buy into the illusion that your life actually is the Pinterest board it looks like, and they eat your cupcakes without gaining a pound, because they believe you have control.

Isn't this the ideal we yearn for? Control over every aspect of our lives—our health, finances, kids, and marriages? Nothing bad would ever happen because we simply wouldn't allow it.

REALITY CHECK

But that isn't real life. Reality hits us when we pull out our daily planners full of careful lists and then are honestly surprised when we can't cross anything off before we go to bed. We expect events to happen in our lives at a certain time and to unfold in a certain way that is predetermined by us. And when things don't happen that way—when we discover that the cupcakes have five hundred calories each—we just might feel as if we're twirling around naked in the middle of the street, screaming at the sky for an explanation.

The fact is that most of us get up every morning with the notion that we are basically in control. Then, on one of those mornings, something happens that shows us we never were. And if we're among those who hold the ideal of control in a death grip, an encounter with reality can leave us lonely, curled up, and crying in a corner (hopefully not in a dirty bathrobe, clutching a bottle of bourbon, and tearing into a bag of chips).

While we're in this self-pity-induced haze, we can't see clearly. The illusion of control steals our joy. Why? you may ask. Because this thief brings along with it two sidekicks known as expectations and comparison. Life brings you situations that are not what you wanted or expected, and it doesn't necessarily bring you what it brings to others. It's like when you order a big, juicy bacon cheeseburger and bite into it, only to discover that someone has substituted turkey bacon and tofu. Meanwhile, the friend you're having lunch with gets exactly what she ordered specifically the way she wanted it. It's just not fair.

Great expectations. We all have them, don't we? I know I did! I planned to get married in my twenties and start a family. I assumed, with extreme confidence, that my future husband and I would picket-fence our lives. We'd buy a charming house in a darling neighborhood and send our genius kids to private school. The kids would be incredibly smart, motivated, and very holy, and our marital relationship would put the greatest love stories to shame.

No, I wasn't a spoiled brat with a big entitlement problem. I just wanted the soaps to be real, except that Frisco would choose me over Felicia. Needless to say, I never met Frisco, and Port Charles was far from my reality. When my expectations were not met, I wasn't angry, just confused—I didn't understand why my plans weren't coming together. But I was still determined to eat the calorie-free cupcake, so I kept on making plans and building expectations and forging ahead. It wasn't until I was married with two children that life's hard truths began to chip away at my allegiance to control.

I guess, in a way, I'm lucky that things fell apart when I was younger, while I could still stay up past ten p.m. and get up at six a.m. without the urge to wear yoga pants all day. Since then, it's taken me a quarter century to come to a place of realistic self-awareness and reliance on the One who truly controls things. But it's not yet time to talk about God. Right now, this story is about me. (It's okay. He and I have chatted about this, and he's okay with it. He knows it's going to be all about him anyway.)

Let's get to the real story. Once upon a time, my husband, Jerry, and I were living out his dream to be a naval aviator. Although it meant long months apart, I happily followed him from duty station to duty station. It was a great adventure where he was the captain and I his first mate. We were a team with a plan. And a plan meant we were in control—until we weren't.

AT THE FONT

"I baptize you in the name of the Father, and of the Son, and of the Holy Spirit," the priest said. "Amen." For Christians, these holy words bring new life. On a crisp Sunday afternoon in September 1992, my non-Catholic husband; three-year-old son, Jonathan; and I stood around the font in the suburban Maryland church that I grew up in as a priest spoke these words over, baptized, and anointed our one-month-old daughter, Courtney Elizabeth.

While the priest did his thing, I made lists in my mental daily planner. I hate to admit it, but this was a get-this-kid-baptized-quickly kind of ceremony. We had a few of my large extended family in attendance, but despite the fact that she wore the family baptismal gown, there would be no party. After the ceremony we were heading back to Maine. Why? Because the following week, the navy was moving us from Maine to Washington, DC. We had a schedule to keep, and there was no room for deviation. That came back to bite me in a big way.

Just as the priest poured holy water over our daughter's head, Courtney arched her back, and her face turned purple. She held her breath and her body jerked once, twice, and a third time. Her movements were so sudden that I almost dropped her. Then she turned into a spaghetti noodle, and I pulled her in close. *What was happening? Was the water too cold? Was it too loud in the church? What was going on?* I glanced at my father and then my husband. Had they seen that? My father, who was fighting cancer at the time, went pale, while my husband's gaze darted around the church like a sniper's on the hunt. My breath caught, and my vision blurred. Something *had* happened. Something was wrong.

POWERLESS

Within the hour, I found myself in an emergency room with our daughter actively seizing. Nurses buzzed around Courtney like bees around a sunflower. It was confusing, disorienting, and just plain scary. Minutes or hours later, a doctor gave our daughter a shot in the thigh, and she went limp in my arms. The doctor took her gently in his arms and disappeared without speaking a word. I didn't know that when he walked away with our daughter, our world would change forever.

The next few hours were hell. By the time we saw Courtney again, the sun had gone down, and the heavy weight of discontent had settled on both Jerry and me. Our tempers were short, and our fear hit the top of the charts. We wanted answers, and no one had them. We heard big, scary terms. Nurses took blood and placed an IV in our daughter's small hand, and doctors ordered an electroencephalogram (EEG) and a spinal tap. There were many tears, both Courtney's and mine.

Looking at her in the hospital crib, I couldn't get over how small she was. Courtney was just a little baby, only five weeks old. Her hand was all bandaged to keep the IV in place, and there were wires poking out from underneath a little hospital gown that had pink elephants on it. Machines hanging over her bed hummed and beeped with regularity.

Every time she had a seizure, alarms rang out and an army of hospital staff came rushing into the room.

The whole thing was overwhelming, and I was losing my grip on my emotions. To make things even worse (because things can *always* get worse), it was well past Jonathan's bedtime. Jerry took our son back to my parents' house so he could leave in the morning to make it to Maine in time to meet the military movers. A terrifying realization set in: not only was I alone but I also had no control over this situation.

As they pushed Courtney's crib down the empty hall in the basement of the hospital, passing one hazardous material sign after another, I heard only silence. They wouldn't let me go back with her; once again I was relegated to the sidelines. I don't like the sidelines. I'm an all-in kind of girl. Since I couldn't participate, I paced the waiting room and prayed. All of my expectations had been doused with lighter fluid and set aflame. I wasn't happy.

And what does an unhappy Mary do? She yells at God: *Don't you dare let her die.*

Then Mary begs: *Please, don't let her die.*

And then Mary makes a deal: *I'll take her any way you wish to give her to me, just don't let her die.*

That night was the beginning of my seven-day vigil in the pediatric intensive care unit (PICU). I never left Courtney's side for one moment that week. I was too afraid something would happen while I was gone. If it had, I knew that I would never forgive myself. At the end of the week, with Courtney still seizing multiple times a day, this was all the doctors could tell me: "Ma'am? We have no idea why your daughter is having seizures." It's hard to describe the utter despair I felt in that moment. Jerry was still in Maine, my son was with my parents, and I was alone.

As the doctors apologized and promised to keep searching for answers, they handed me prescription drugs and gave me instructions on how to care for Courtney. All I could hear was my own internal shouts into an eternal silence. *God hadn't heard my screams and cries or taken me up on any of my bargains*, I thought. Once the doctors left, I fell to my knees and wept. I knew what was happening: God was punishing me.

PERFECT

I once heard it said that to have children is to allow your heart to walk outside your body. It's a vulnerable and trusting act to bring a child into the world, and Jerry and I had done that twice now. What we had not told anyone was that the week before this horrific turn of events, I'd had my tubes tied at the age of twenty-five. Despite the Church's teaching on being open to life, Jerry and I had decided that we were done having babies. There were too many variables at play—from my difficult pregnancies to his desire for a very small family—for us to take any chances. We wanted to be in control of our own destinies, and we were happy with one boy and one girl. Two perfect children for our perfect life.

But our perfect life was circling the drain, and panicked questions taunted me. Was God angry? Was he taking revenge because we had closed ourselves to the future gift of children? Was Courtney going to die?

I felt terrified and confused and betrayed. In my mind, our situation confirmed that God was a tyrant. I felt just like I had in grade school when I was sent to the principal's office for breaking a rule, except now my daughter was paying the price. There isn't a word in the dictionary to define my anger that day. All my life I had been taught that Jesus had come to save us by suffering for us on the Cross. Yet now, he was allowing Courtney to suffer. What was *that* about?

I have to be honest: at this point in my life, I thought God was a bully. I had not felt his love or experienced his mercy. I was still determined to solve the problem, to find a way to fix all of this somehow. Surrender was not an option, just a sign of weakness—and I *had* to be strong. If God wouldn't help me, I'd do it myself.

I can hear your laughter from here. Yes, I had much to learn. I got on my knees deeply angry with God. I unleashed my fear and anxiety and gave him my complete and honest opinion of the current situation. Because Jerry wasn't Catholic and had a very loose relationship with God, I felt utterly alone in this. I knew that if either of us was going to pray, it would have to be me and me alone. Luckily, God is as gracious as he is loving, and he didn't give up on me. In the midst of my silent screams, I felt a slight shift in my heart, like a hiccup of time, a moment of calm in the middle of one hell of a storm. I took a breath and God spoke words into my heart. I'll be forever grateful to the Holy Spirit for allowing me to hear them: *I love her. She belongs to me. And she's perfect just as she is.*

God saw Courtney and loved her just as she was. In the midst of the chaos and the suffering, he saw perfection and claimed our daughter for his own.

AN INVITATION

I've been a Catholic all my life. In my early years, I thought Jesus was a superhero, better than Superman. When I became a teenager, God became a rule maker and stern disciplinarian, just like Sr. Mercita ("Looks like a cheetah and growls like one too," we used to say about the nun at our school). God's voice was not merciful but full of judgment. My relationship with God had never matured beyond that between Almighty Creator and whiny, entitled teenager.

As I traveled through those seven endless days yelling at, begging, and bargaining with God, I realized that he was inviting me to grow up and form a new relationship with him. I kept running across the Bible verse from Jeremiah that stated, "For I know well the plans I have in mind for you—oracle of the LORD—plans for your welfare and not for woe, so as to give you a future of hope" (29:11). Friends had quoted that scripture to me all week long, it was on the parish bulletin my mom gave me when she brought Jonathan to visit us that week, and it was even engraved on a bracelet one of the PICU nurses was wearing. God was desperately trying to get my attention—I could not escape it. He wasn't punishing me or Jerry; he was allowing a situation that was somehow going to bring "a future of hope." He was asking me to trust him with my beautiful newborn daughter.

That's bananas. Crazy town. Insanity.

I'm not a big fan of suffering or pain and not particularly willing to accept misery and sorrow. And trusting in someone or something makes us vulnerable. In the past, every time I'd ever laid my vulnerability on the table, things had worsened. I felt like I was playing *Frogger*: fulfilling

God's ask was like trying to cross a superhighway, dodging and weaving through the speeding cars. It was too much, and I couldn't do it.

Then I remembered the desperate deal I'd offered: *I'll take her any way you wish to give her to me, just don't let her die.* See where this is going? God had allowed Courtney to live. Awesome. He'd also allowed her to seize uncontrollably for no apparent reason. (Insert bad word here.) That's when I figured it out: if God was going to hold up his end of the "deal," then I had to keep mine. That meant that I'd have to trust him with my daughter's life and, as a bonus with purchase, my own.

It was seven days and nights before I managed to accept the deal I thought I was making. (I've since learned that things don't work this way when you're dealing with an almighty divinity who loves you eternally. God keeps his word, even when we don't.) God wasn't interested in extracting anything from me; he wanted me to trust him and to embrace his plan for our family, especially regarding my daughter. Once we dip a toe into this pond of trust and enter into a deeper relationship, God will ask a lot from us. He does this because he knows what we are capable of even when we don't. He wants us to trust him completely, not because it's good for him but because it's best for us. Trust gives us the grace we need to walk in faith that all shall be well. And when we don't trust, the lessons get harder and longer. Just ask me how I know.

I went all in with no idea where it would lead. In hindsight, this was a good thing. I had no idea what God would ask of me, but it hurt less to trust and surrender than to reach for control and be fearful. Some say (mothers and nuns, mostly) that a person will change only when the pain of staying in the same situation is greater than the perceived pain of change. I can attest to this truth. In that moment, I told God "enough" and laid down my heart, trusting, briefly, that he wouldn't crush it. At times, I still struggle with trust; I am not who I was, but God is not finished with me yet.

HEART WORK

What about you? We all suffer. We all have struggles in our life, events that strip away our sense of control. But since control is an illusion, seeking it is essentially a giant neon sign saying you don't trust God to do what's best for you. I'm not talking about a menu plan for the week or your daily carpool schedule, although God can speak into those things as well.

When the big ask comes and you find yourself on your knees, completely unsure of what will happen with your next breath, your heart shattering into a million pieces and seized by indecision over the right thing to do, you have St. Paul's assurance that God will work all things together for the good of those who love him (see Romans 8:28). That doesn't mean that every last thing will be good. It means that as God works all things together, he will bring about what is good for you. And it won't necessarily be "good" the way you see it, but it will be the way God sees it.

How do we trust God? Hard work, my friend, and a little bit of heart work as well.

Have you ever had an experience where you felt helpless, alone, and scared that nothing would ever be the same? Take out your journal, the notes app on your phone, a napkin (preferably not one from a bar), or use the next page in this book. Start writing. Get it out of your head and in front of your heart. Ask yourself:

- *How is God allowing me to break today?*
- *What is he asking of me?*
- *What do I need to lay down at the foot of the Cross and allow his mercy and grace to seep into?*

Write it out. Draw it out. Give it to him. When we give our very selves, our children, our marriages, and our work over to God, miracles happen, peace abides, and we can be brave in the scared. We can survive the very worst that life brings us, and we can even do it with joy, because "for God all things are possible" (Mt 19:26).

MATTHEW 7:7-11

Ask, and it will be given to you; seek and you will find; knock and the door will be opened to you. For everyone who asks, receives; and the one who seeks, finds; and to the one who knocks, the door will be opened. Which one of you would hand his son a stone when he asks for a loaf of bread, or a snake when he asks for a fish? If you then, who are wicked, know how to give good gifts to your children, how much more will your heavenly Father give good things to those who ask him.

Mary Lenaburg is a full-time Catholic speaker and author of *Be Brave in the Scared*, which earned a 2020 Excellence in Publishing Award from the Association of Catholic Publishers.

She has given keynotes at conferences internationally, including the Edel Gathering, the Genius Women's Conference, the Fiat Conference, Military Council for Catholic Women European Retreat, and the Women of the Word Conference. A writer with Take Up & Read, Lenaburg's work has appeared in five of their meditation books. She has also contributed to two other books.

She has appeared on Catholic radio, TV, and podcasts, including *The Jennifer Fulwiler Show*, *EWTN Pro-Life Weekly*, *The Hallie Lord Show*, *The Gist*, *Busted Halo*, and *Fountains of Carrots*. Lenaburg serves her home parish in many roles, including catechist, sacristan, and extraordinary minister of Holy Communion.

She and her husband, Jerry, live in Fairfax, Virginia, with their son, Jonathan. Their daughter, Courtney, passed away in 2014.

Facebook: **marylenaburgwriter**
Instagram: **@marylenaburg**
Pinterest: **@Mary Lenaburg**
Twitter: **@marylenaburg**
YouTube: **shorturl.at/rzI28**
Patreon: **shorturl.at/pvS08**

Leah Darrow is a Catholic speaker, podcaster, author, and the founder of Lux U.